HOW TO
WRITE
AND GIVE
A GOOD TALK

CAMERON REID ARMSTRONG

Pimpernel Press
Provo, Utah

Cameron Reid Armstrong
Pimpernel Press 2023

Names: Armstrong, Cameron Reid, Author.
Title: How to Write And Give A Good Talk / Cameron Reid Armstrong.
Discription: Provo, Utah: Pimpernell Press, [2023] Includes Bibliographical references.

Summary: "Cameron Reid Armstrong writes about the mindsets and principles for writing and giving a good talk for members of the Church of Jesus Christ of Latter-day Saints applying principles of public speaking to our Sacrament Services. The author uses personal examples of those principles in action or experiences he has witnessed from others" - Provided by publisher

Courtney Larkin Editing https://larkinediting.com
Photo: Brian Walker

ISBN # 979-8-9879812-0-7 (Paperback)

First Edition 2023

To my wife Connie, my rock.
Who has been patient beyond belief with my writing projects.

The hardest thing for a writer's spouse to understand
is when they are staring out the window they are working.

A big thank you too:
The Breakfast Club, you know who you are.
This would not have happened without your feedback,
encouragement, and accountability.

And Finally, To my Parents:
Who taught me the gospel and that I could do hard things like
pulling weeds, moving to Egypt, and speaking in public

Deb,
Thank you again for
your feedback on this book.
you were a great help on the internal
information and the formating.
A few books you recomended helped
with formating. I know you dont
need this book but you get one for
helping.

*"All the great speakers
were bad speakers at first"*
-Ralph Waldo Emerson

*"Without new experiences,
something inside us sleeps.
The sleeper must awaken"*
– Frank Herbert

Table of Contents

Introduction

Picture, if you will, a light fall evening. You and your family are settling down for a hard-earned dinner after a long day of work and school. The twin four-year-olds are fighting again, but it's not severe, and they look so cute. Your twelve-year-old son is home for once and not at his friend's house, and your nine-year-old daughter is actually talking to you after you, apparently very rudely, asked her to clean her room yesterday. You're tired yet grateful for this family time. Suddenly the classic 1977 song Staying Alive starts to play from your pocket, and you reluctantly take out your phone.

"Who could that be?" your spouse asks.

"Must be a telemarketer," you reply. "They always call during dinnertime." You look down and check the number. Your posture stiffens, and your family becomes concerned at your sudden silence. Several ethical dilemmas begin to challenge your conscience.

This number is not a telemarketer; it belongs to a neighbor who lives down the street—he is also the first counselor in the bishopric of your ward...

Three minutes later you are gasping at the words that have just left your mouth: "Sure, I can speak this coming Sunday, no problem." Your family looks at you in silence; your spouse is impressed, and your kids are amazed at your bravery in following inspiration to do hard things. Your twelve-year-old leans over to you and says, "My teacher told us a joke from Jerry Seinfeld? 'According to most studies, people's number one fear is public speaking. Number two is death. Death is number two? Does that sound right? This means to the average person, if you go to a funeral, you're better off in the casket than delivering the eulogy,'" and then belts out a non-sympathetic laugh.

You begin dishing up the food, as you want to enjoy this time with your family, yet your mind is already wondering how to begin the process. It was three years ago when you last spoke in church, and you would welcome a little help: tips for public speaking, warnings of the traps you may fall into, an example outline to use, and how to create crisp stories and examples. If you only had some sort of resource to look through later on, you may get to enjoy this family time.

Well, here you go!

This book offers that little bit of help you are asking for. To help you get over that number-one fear and to allow death its true place. Public speaking does not have to be your favorite thing to do, but can be something you are not afraid to do.

Preparing to speak in church can provide wonderful opportunities for learning, growing, and coming closer to Christ, and your talk can have a positive influence on your congregation— maybe even change someone's life.

The Lord wants you to be an instrument in his hands.

How to Use This Book

This book is designed with short chapters that build on each other, but each chapter can stand on its own. Read straight through, or skip around to topics you are interested in or known weaknesses.

The structure of each chapter is an example of how to use the principles of organization; if you find one you like, you can use that same pattern yourself. I also include several general conference talks you can use as examples, and I outline the principles they use.

The main goals of this book are the following:

- To improve your attitude and mindset about public speaking

- To give you examples of ways to be more confident in your abilities

- To help you avoid things that are unnecessary for the talk or distracting to the congregation

- To remind you to draw upon the grace of Jesus Christ as you attempt something you may believe beyond your ability

You've Got This!

*"All speaking is public speaking,
whether it's to one person
or a thousand."*
- Roger Love

*A wise man speaks because he has something to say;
a fool speaks because he has to say something."*
-Plato

Part 1:
Essential Mindsets
To Start With

Your mindset is the default way you view and make sense of the world. Living by a mindset helps your brain not have to think or process as much; you simply react according to your mindset, whether that be optimistic, pessimistic, etc. Your mindset helps to save mental energy. You can change your default setting, but it takes willingness, effort, and intent. Mindset can be broken down into two types: growth mindset or fixed mindset.

When it comes to giving a talk in church, ask yourself these questions:

- Am I fixed in my thinking and behavior so I end up giving my talk the same as everyone else?

- Am I willing to look for growth and find new and different ways to share my message?

Part 1 holds key principles in developing a growth mindset, both for giving a talk in church and growing in other parts of your life.

1

Intent

*"You can speak well
if your tongue can deliver
the message of your heart."*
-John Ford

Years ago, my boss asked if we could talk privately when things slowed down. I told him, "Sure thing." I, unfortunately, already knew the topic of this conversation: I was not doing my best at work. He knew it, and so did I. Although the next two hours were busy, I found myself coming up with every reason, justification, and rationale to convince myself that he was the one that was wrong. In fact, I was so convinced my behavior was acceptable that I grew angry at the things I predicted he was going to say.

The time came for me to go steaming-mad into this conversation, but Rick caught me off guard when he started the conversation like this: "Hey, Cameron, thanks for coming in; tell me, when are midterms?" I stumbled for a second and then said, "They're in a month." He nodded his head and then asked, "How are your parents?" I looked at him puzzled then responded, "They're fine, thanks for asking." He then asked me about my current girlfriend, my car, my band (I'm a drummer), and other activities that I enjoyed outside of work and school.

I answered all the questions he proposed to me and then asked one of my own: "So…why did you want to meet with me?"

He replied, "I've noticed that your work has been off these past few weeks. You haven't been yourself, so I figured something must be going on in your life, and I just wanted to see if I could help."

The next words that came out of my mouth surprised me. I said, "Actually, Rick, I've just been kind of lazy these last few weeks. I want to apologize about that, and I promise I will step things up, you will see a difference."

Rick then said, "Well, if that's the only issue then I believe you; let's get back to work." I left that conversation both confused at what had just happened and more committed than ever to work harder for Rick.

What caused this change in me? Rick's secret was his intent. He was not focused on performance, quotas, or anything work-related—he was focused on me and me alone, and his intent was to help. His intent was so powerful that it actually snuffed out my anger and inspired the best behavior out of me, even when I was determined to do the exact opposite. His intent was everything, and it showed so much that I ended up changing.

Have you ever considered your intent when giving a talk? We can prepare our talks to address the assigned topic, yet, in the back of our minds, we really hope to impress everyone with our wit and wisdom. We may want to do a good job, but, in the back of our minds, we don't like public speaking and just want to get it over with quickly. Unfortunately, these intentions come across to the audience even if we don't think they do. When we give a talk with a "sincere heart, with real intent, having faith in Christ"[1] the Spirit can do its work, and we can become instruments in His hands.

Our intent has everything to do with who we are inside, and it will eventually affect what we do on the outside. For Rick, our conversation was grounded in his intent to help, not in trying to manipulate me into working harder, and, for this reason, he inspired change.

Just as Rick's intent was rooted in helping, our intent as we prepare and give talks should be similarly rooted in the right thing. Elder Boyd K. Packer said, "[The Atonement of Christ] is the very root of Christian doctrine. You may know much about the gospel as it branches out from there, but if you only know the branches and those branches do not touch that root, if they have been cut free from that truth, there will be no life nor substance nor redemption in them"[2].

4

I have to admit that I have given many talks that were not touching that root, and, even though they may have been entertaining or motivational, they lacked truth, life, substance, and redemption. If our real intent is to bring others to Christ, then we must let that root branch out and shape our actions as we prepare what the Lord would have us say. We can turn our sacrament meetings into revelatory experiences of conversion.

Giving a talk is a perfect time to demonstrate how gospel principles and the grace of Christ can be applied not just in our daily lives but also in the present moment as we are giving our talk. We can apply Paul's admonition: "Be thou an example of the believers, in word, in conversation, in charity, in spirit, in faith, in purity"[3]. What was it that inspired me to give Rick the exact answer I wanted to hide from him? It was his authenticity, humility, and connection. In short, it was his pure intent.

Nephi was firm and direct in his purpose for writing on plates: "For the fulness of mine intent is that I may persuade men to come unto the God of Abraham, and the God of Isaac, and the God of Jacob, and be saved"[4]. He continues, "For we labor diligently to write, to persuade our children, and also our brethren, to believe in Christ, and to be reconciled to God"[5].

You don't need to state your intent out loud, but consider your intent as you prepare, and always have the same goal in mind as Nephi and Moroni—to invite everyone to "come unto Christ, and be perfected in him"[6]

As John Ford said, "You can speak well if your tongue can deliver the message of your heart." All you really need is for your heart to be in the right place, and then your message will match it. You don't have to do it alone though. Elder Jeffrey R. Holland clarifies how intent works and where help can come from. He taught, "The scriptures phrase such earnest desire as being of 'real intent,' pursued 'with full purpose of heart, acting no hypocrisy and no deception before God.' I testify that in response to that kind of importuning, God will send help from both sides of the veil"[7]

5

Small Summary -Consider your intent from the start-	
Avoid These Traps	Try These Tips
1. *Writing a talk on your own wisdom and agenda can eventually leave you standing at the pulpit alone, with no spirit to help testify*	1. *Ask for heaven's help; ask, "what should I speak about?" Who am I addressing?" and "What should I say?"*
2. *A focus to only entertain or motivate can lack truth, life, substance, and redemption.*	2. *Relate back to Christ and His grace to give your talk life, substance, and redemption*
3. *The desire to be funny or to impress will eventually come to the forefront in your behavior and attitude so make sure you know what your full intent is*	3. *Authenticity, humility, and connection inspire change in others*

References/Resources:

1. Moroni 10:4

2. Ensign, May 1977, "The Mediator," Boyd K. Packer, BYU Speeches, 2006, "The Very Root of Christian Doctrine" Thomas B Griffith

3. 1 Timothy 4:12

4. 1 Nephi 6:4

5. 2 Nephi 25:23

6. Moroni 10:32

7. Ensign, May 2013, "Lord I Believe" Jeffrey R. Holland

8. Ensign, October 2011, "Speaking in Sacrament Meeting?" John Hilton III and Mindy Raye Friedman

9. Ensign, May 2017, "Drawing the Power of Jesus Christ into Our Lives," Russell M. Nelson

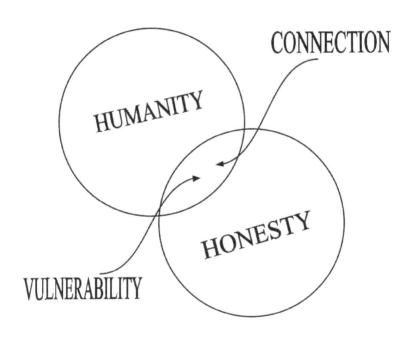

Embracing Vulnerability

A powerful moment in sports history happened during the 1996 Olympics and was done by one of the greatest athletes ever. However, it was not on a court, a track, a pool, or a podium; it happened in a space that was about a five-foot radius, and all he did was stand.

The '96 summer Olympics was held in Atlanta, Georgia, USA, and the question that was on everyone's minds was, "Who is lighting the torch?" Lighting the torch is the greatest honor, and this time it was a closely guarded secret. Even Bob Costas, the legendary broadcaster, didn't know who it was; Dick Ebersol said to him, "I am not going to tell you who it is, you will instantly recognize him or her, but I want your reaction to be as spontaneous as everyone else in the stadium." When the time came and the man stepped out from the shadow, there was an audible gasp from the crowd, followed a few seconds later by thunderous applause as they saw Muhammad Ali—the greatest boxer of all time—waiting to receive the flame. As Muhammad Ali lit his torch with the torch of Janet Evens, the crowd could easily see that he was shaking uncontrollably. He was not shaking with excitement or trepidation, but from the brutal effects of Parkinson's disease which had taken away his ability to control his own limbs and rendered him unable to speak. As he did his best, struggling through the ceremony, and eventually lighting the Olympic torch, the crowd continued to patiently cheer[1].

In a 2022 interview, Bob Costas identifies that seeing the humanity of Muhammad Ali was what made that moment so powerful; he stated,

> Here was [Muhammad Ali], once the most beautiful and most nimble of athletes, who was a beautiful figure in a brutal sport. He was willing to present himself shaking and trembling, such a contrast to his former self… and yet he was willing… to present himself to the world that way. It was poignant, it was profound, and I think everybody got it, in their own way, everybody got it. I get goosebumps still thinking about it, the humanity of it… throughout his life, this man put his money where his mouth was, this guy walked the walk, he put it all on the line, you got to respect that"[2].

I also remember seeing that event live on TV, and it will always be a sacred and special memory. The humanity of seeing one of the greatest at his weakest, and his willingness to stand shaking in front of the entire world is engraved on my memory; I still get goosebumps thinking about it.

We can take this example and the effect it had on the crowd and apply it to our future speaking experience: how do we show our humanity to the congregation? You may think, "Sometimes I am also trembling at the microphone, but it's because I am so nervous. Muhammad Ali couldn't help it, but what if I can't help it either, and the congregation sees me being nervous?"

I answer that question by saying, "Let them see." If they know we are vulnerable, while also not giving excuses, then they will do something you may not believe—they will not judge us; they will cheer for us to do well, and they will pay more attention.

Let me explain this further. Tony Bennett's lesson from Frank Sinatra is a story of allowing others to see your vulnerability. He states,

> I was pretty frightened because I was still pretty new… I took a chance and met Sinatra backstage and he was nice enough to have me up in his dressing room. [Frank] asked me, 'What's the matter kid?' I said, 'I was very nervous performing' and he said, 'Don't worry about that, if

the public senses that you're nervous they will support you even more and you will find out it is one of the best things that could ever happen.' Sure enough, it relaxed me for the rest of my life on the stage… It was a great lesson[3].

A modern-day example of this principle is from a talk (one of my favorites of all time) given by a woman in my home ward. She was assigned the topic of the Atonement of Jesus Christ, and we could tell she was overwhelmed.

She started her talk with a statement like this (not as a disclaimer, but with confidence): "I didn't know how to write this talk, but I prepared one anyway. As I studied the Atonement and the grace that comes from it, I realized that his grace could help me prepare, and when the time came, He would help me give it." Now, could there ever be a better living sermon on the grace that comes from Jesus Christ? Like Mohamid Ali, she was willing to be vulnerable, with no excuses, and we were fixed on her; we leaned in, and we supported her. When she finished it was a loud, reverent, and unanimous, "Amen," the kind you know that everyone in attendance participated in. Years later, when I remind people of this talk, many say, "Yes, I remember that; I will never forget it." This is the power of vulnerability. If you are nervous, let them know; the congregation will not judge you, and they will support you.[4]

Brené Brown, the premier researcher on vulnerability, spoke of the need for more vulnerability. She said,

> We need more people who are willing to demonstrate what it looks like to risk and endure failure, disappointment, and regret—people willing to feel their own hurt instead of working it out on other people, people willing to own their stories, live their values and keep showing up[5].

She also notes that being vulnerable is not excruciating, yet it is also not comfortable. But if you want to unlock the full power of vulnerability and connect with your congregation, then you must look at it as necessary. Your example can be a living testimony that inspires your audience to also ask for God's help in the hard parts of their lives.

11

Small Summary *-Vulnerability inspires others and shows strength-*	
Avoid These Traps	Try These Tips
• *Excluding any vulnerability creates an emotionless talk.*	• *Showing your humanity will create a connection with the congregation.*
• *Making disclaimers only lowers the congregation's expectations*	• *Appropriate disclosure shows the congregation your faith*
• *Focusing on what you think they think of you causes you to close up*	• *Allowing the congregation to see your struggles inspires their engagement and support*
• *Focusing on your weaknesses will unconsciously focus on the congregation's as well*	• *Being an in-the-moment example of Christ's grace will grow the congregation's faith*

References/Resources:

1. YouTube: Gold Medal Moments: Muhammad Ali @ Atlanta 1996 Games Opening Ceremony

2. YouTube: In Depth With Graham Bensinger: Bob Costas: Muhammad Ali, Feb 23, 2022

3. YouTube: Tony Bennett on seeing Frank Sinatra at the Paramount Theater in New York

4. See Part Two: Disclaimers Discredit You

5. Brené Brown, 2015, "Rising Strong"

God Uses the Weak
and Simple of the Earth

"I do not glory of myself, but I glory
in that which the Lord hath commanded me;...
that perhaps I may be an instrument in the hands of God."
- <u>Alma 29:9</u>

While I was in college, a friend offered me a chance to interview at a garage that performed automobile services. I was a bit nervous because I knew nothing about cars. My friend said to me, "Make sure you say that in the interview; it will be an advantage for you." I was confused, but I did as I was told. When I met with Rick, the manager, I told him I knew nothing about cars and his response surprised me: he said, "That makes you more qualified; now I can easily teach you my way of doing things rather than starting with unlearning the way you did it at another garage."

As I pondered this concept, I eventually realized a gospel pattern of why the Lord chooses the weak, simple, and unlearned to assist in his work. He wants to teach them His ways right away and not have to start with unlearning other patterns. When the Lord chooses unlearned people like Joseph Smith, it is easy for us to see the hand of the Lord because there are no other explanations for what happened. If the Lord had picked the best author or linguist at the time to translate the Book of Mormon, then it would be hard to believe it really was translated by the gift and power of God. The Lord truly meant it when he stated, "For I will show unto the children of men that I am able to do mine own work"[2].

If you truly do not believe you are competent or capable to speak in church or perform any other calling, then you are now fully qualified to be an instrument in the hand of God. The best talks are not given by those who are the best speakers. The best speakers can be too confident and don't look to the Lord for help. Those that look to the Lord are the ones that can really have an impact; they can be living examples of faith in Christ and be "led by the Spirit, not knowing beforehand the things which [they] should do"[3].

A brother or sister asking for the grace of Christ to help them during their talk, a teen asking the faith of the congregation to be united with theirs, or someone starting a new job who knows nothing about cars are all in a perfect state of humility to be shaped by the One who knows best and to become what the master intended them to be: instruments in His hands.

Small Summary
-Not feeling qualified humbles us, and then God qualifies us-

Avoid These Traps	Try These Tips
• *You don't ask for the Lord's help; you believe you can do it on your own* • *You listen to your negative thoughts of "I'm not qualified"* • *You don't believe the Lord's blessings apply to you personally*	• *God taught Nephi how to build a ship. God can teach you how to write your talk* • *Humility is the key; the best talks are not by the best speakers* • *Sinners can be instruments too; let the master shape you*

16

References/Resources:

1. Alma 29:9
2. 2 Nephi 27:21
3. 1 Nephi 4:6

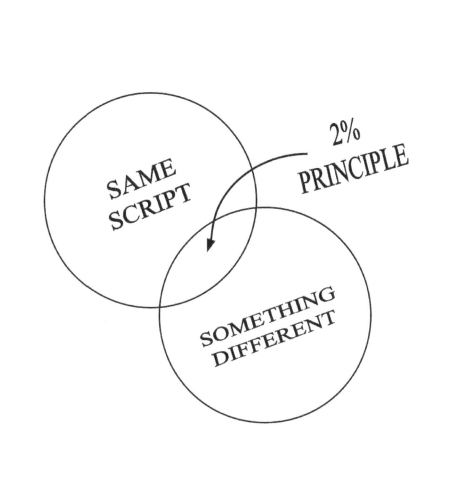

Change the Script - The 2% Principle

"Meeting expectations is good.
Exceeding expectations is better…
Exceeding expectations is where satisfaction ends
and loyalty begins."
-Ron Kaufman

I enjoy going out for breakfast and getting a bottomless-french toast platter. Oddly enough, at one restaurant it comes with a small plastic cup of syrup that is never enough. Sometimes I ask for an extra one from the start yet many times I forget and have to ask later. Once, after they brought me out my plate and the small cup of syrup, I was preparing to go into the usual script of asking for more and expecting to hear the usual response back to me, "I can do that, no problem." But this time the server came back with two more plastic cups of syrup and said, "Just in case." I thought this was amazing; it was a fresh surprise, and it was only a small gesture from our server. You see, good customer service means consistently meeting customers' known script. But great customer service can be described just like our church talks ought to be: quick, simple, personalized, and empathetic. We should know what is expected of us and change the script.

But what percentage does the script need to be changed… 10%, or 50%, to make a lasting impression? The script only needs to be changed by 2%. Think of how hard it was to bring me two more cups of syrup. About 2% more effort on the servers' part, and yet it made a lasting impression.

Whenever people get more than what they expect, no matter the amount, they are either blown away, feel lucky, or are grateful. All you need to do is know the script of what is expected of you and change 2%; the result could be similar to me getting two more cups of syrup, and the experience would be heightened for your congregation.

Those who have been going to sacrament services of a Latter-day Saint congregation will know the usual script that is part of a sacrament meeting talk, including some of the following:

• The story of how you were asked to give the talk

• A disclaimer of some sort: "I'm not really the best person for this topic…"

• A joke at the start of a talk in an attempt to loosen the crowd (yet it actually loses them)

• Telling people what your topic is

Since we know the script and what is typically expected, we can now prepare to exceed the usual expectations listeners have and give them the extra 2% they were not expecting.

For ideas see Part Three: Invite Revelation and Testify, and Part Four: Crafting Examples that Focus on the Message.

Throughout this book, with each concept of public speaking, each trap, and each tip, I will leave small blank lines for you to write your own thoughts and revelations on that extra 2% you could do differently to shift your talk away from the normal script.

Write down the typical things you expect to hear from speakers in your ward. _____

_____

_____

_____

_____

_____

_____

_____

_____

_____

The 2% Principle:

In my next talk or testimony I will exceed expectations by _____

_____
_____
_____
_____
_____
_____
_____
_____

Small Summary *-Exceed expectations and heighten the experience by 2%-*	
Avoid These Traps	Try These Tips
• *The usual and unoriginally scripted openers including unnecessary stories, disclaimers, or jokes*	• *Start off with a well crafted story to draw them in*
• *Follow the script and possibly lose the audience before you start*	• *Change the script and they will be blown away, feel lucky, or be grateful*
• *Be like everyone else; be remembered like everyone else*	• *They will remember the differences in your talk, and you can have influence*

"I must not fear.
Fear is the mind-killer.
Fear is the little-death that brings total obliteration.
I will face my fear.
I will permit it to pass over me and through me.
And when it has gone past I will turn the inner eye to see its path.
Where the fear has gone there will be nothing.
Only I will remain."
*– **Frank Herbert***

"You gain strength, courage, and confidence
by every experience in which you really
stop to look fear in the face."
*– **Eleanor Roosevelt***

Part 2:
Overcoming Fear

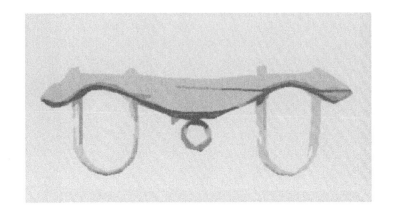

"Take My Yoke Upon You"
Mathew 11:28

The Grace of Christ

"Yea, ye do stand well,
as if ye were supported by the hand of a god."
-Giddianhi: leader of the band of robbers[1]

In 1975, while shooting the movie Jaws, director Steven Spielberg encountered budget issues and many struggles with the mechanical shark. This left him to make some hard decisions like not showing the shark on screen as often as he wanted. Even though he didn't plan on it, not having the shark on screen contributed to Jaws being one of the scariest films of its time. Speilberg learned he didn't need to be the one to scare the audience. Not showing the shark left everything up to the imagination of the audience and they could scare themselves much better than he ever could.

When it comes to public speaking, we often fight our imagination more than anything else. Once activated, our "what if" scenarios, unrealistic comparisons to others, and fear of failure start to creep in. In the end, we wind up scaring ourselves much worse than anyone else could.

Elder Kevin W. Pearson taught us, "Faith and fear cannot coexist. One gives way to the other. The simple fact is we all need to constantly build faith and overcome sources of destructive disbelief"[2]. Acting with faith in Christ is a real and tangible force that comes from the performance of

His Atonement. This power is called Christ's grace; we can be filled with it and "do all things through Christ which strengtheneth [us]"[3]. The Bible dictionary defines grace as a "divine means of help or strength, given through the bounteous mercy and love of Jesus Christ"[4].

We can use His grace as we prepare our talk and especially while we give our talk. We may feel alone and anxious at the desk or at the pulpit microphone; yet the Lord can be with us no matter where we are. Paul stated it this way: "At my first answer no man stood with me, but all men forsook me… Notwithstanding the Lord stood with me, and strengthened me; that by me the preaching might be fully known, and that all the Gentiles might hear"[5].

The key to using Christ's grace is to specifically look to and petition the source of the power; in other words, ask for it: "Come unto Christ, and partake of the goodness of God"[6]. Elder Dallin H. Oaks taught:

> Because of His atoning experience in mortality, our Savior is able to comfort, heal, and strengthen all men and women everywhere, but I believe He does so only for those who seek Him and ask for His help. The Apostle James taught, 'Humble yourselves in the sight of the Lord, and he shall lift you up' (James 4:10). We qualify for that blessing when we believe in Him and pray for His help[7].

A youth in my ward spoke of being in gymnastic competitions and how these times strengthened his testimony. Before and after each competition, it was important for him to pray, yet the most important times to pray were when he was worried, afraid, or nervous. Each time he asked for strength or peace during the competition, it would come to him, and he was able to do his best. His example shows how we are not alone in anything we do; Christ's grace is always available to those who ask, whenever they ask, whether at home, at school, or at play.

How does this grace work? Coming unto Him allows you and Christ to work together, equally yoked, as you perform the task you have before you. A yoke is a large wooden tool used as two oxen pull a load; it helps them work together and distributes the weight equally. Christ said, "Come unto me, all ye that labour and are heavy laden, and I will give you rest. Take my yoke upon you, and learn of me; for I am meek and lowly in heart: and ye shall find rest unto your souls"[8].

Elder David A. Bednar gives us a scriptural insight into the ability to handle and overcome our fears as we focus on Christ to find relief and rest. He taught:

> In the land of Helam, Alma's people were frightened by an advancing Lamanite army. "But Alma went forth and stood among them, and exhorted them that they should not be frightened, but … should remember the Lord their God and he would deliver them. Therefore they hushed their fears" (Mosiah 23:27–28). Notice Alma did not hush the people's fears. Rather, Alma counseled the believers to remember the Lord and the deliverance only He could bestow (2 Nephi 2:8). And knowledge of the Savior's protecting watchcare enabled the people to hush their own fears[9].

The Nephites did not wallow in the "what if" scenarios of their imagination, nor did they wait for the battle to start; they looked for Christ's grace and deliverance right away, and through his enabling power, they "hushed their fears" better than anyone else could.

Lachoneus, the governor of the Nephites, received a threatening letter from the leader of the band of robbers, and he responded by thinking of the grace of Christ: "He did cause that his people should cry unto the Lord for strength against the time that the robbers should come down against them"[10].

Next time you are asked to speak, rather than struggling in your imagination with self-doubt, pause for a moment and ask the Lord to help you be humble, teachable, and to grant you His power; you will be amazed at what you can do together. These are the experiences when you, and your testimony of God's hand in your life can be strengthened.

The 2% Principle:

For my next talk I will _____

_____

_____

_____

_____

_____

_____

_____

Small Summary *-Faith and fear cannot coexist. One gives way to the other-*	
Avoid These Traps	Try These Tips
• *Letting your imagination scare you with "what if" scenarios* • *Focusing more on story rather than a message* • *Your fear can to be a tool of the adversary*	• *You can ask for His power specifically and feel His grace at the moment you give your talk* • *Truly believe you can "do all things through Christ"* • *You can "hush your own fears" with Christ's grace*

References/Resources:

1. 3 Nephi 3:2

2. Ensign, May 2009, "Faith in the Lord Jesus Christ," Elder Kevin W. Pearson

3. Philippians 4:13

4. Bible Dictionary: Grace

5. 2 Timothy 4:16-17

6. Jacob 1:7

7. Ensign, November 2015, "Strengthened by the Atonement of Jesus Christ," Elder Dallin H. Oaks

8. Matthew 11:28-30

9. Ensign, May 2015 "Therefore They Hushed Their Fears," Elder David A. Bednar

10. 3 Nephi 3:12

11. BYUI Devotional, January, 2002, "In the Strength of the Lord" David A. Bednar

28

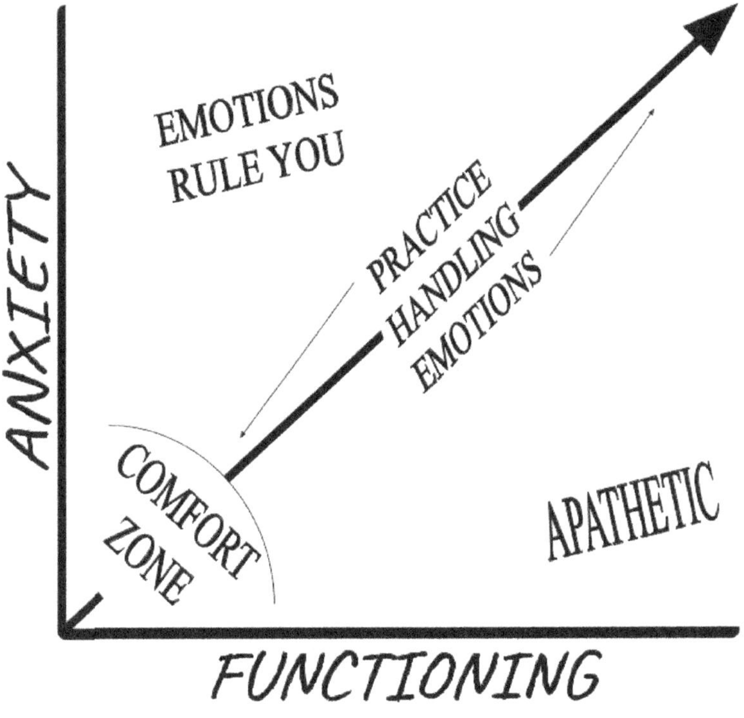

EMOTIONS
RULE YOU
PRACTICE
HANDLING
EMOTIONS
COMFORT
ZONE
APATHETIC
ANXIETY
FUNCTIONING

Achieving Ability Amongst Anxiety

*"There is no place that God cannot go,
especially with a willing,
half-scared-to-death,
ill-equipped vessel."*
-Beth Moore

Would it be hard for you to believe that pro football Hall of Famer Steve Young's anxiety was so difficult for him to control that it was widely known throughout the whole organization? He simply could not hide it. His teammates actually looked forward to his anxiety, teasing that if Steve threw up before a game, it meant he was going to play well. Anxiety was something Steve had to worry about his whole life; in fact, he never spent a night away from home until his first night in the freshman dorms at BYU. Steve has a quote that I love: "Performance is performance and there are pressures that come with it. Anxiety and performance aren't friends"[1]. This is a great insight into the mind of Steve Young. No matter how much he prepared or how much good feedback he got, it was never enough to relieve the anxiety; yet somehow his anxiety never prevented him from going out there and doing his best. Believe him though, for years his anxiety tried its best to stop him.

We are not asked to take on the same pressures as an NFL quarterback, yet the principles taught by Steve Young's example are what we can use to successfully tackle any anxiety in any aspect of our lives[2].

When we have the opportunity to speak in church it can also raise a lot of anxiety in us, yet we can use these opportunities to call on the strength of the Lord and expand our comfort zones.

Nephi was totally pushed out of his comfort zone when he was asked to build a ship, but the way he approached the task gives us something to strongly think about. His faith in God's power and knowledge that it was available to him personally sets a powerful example for us. He said to his brothers,

> If God... should command me that I should say unto this water, be thou earth, it should be earth; and if I should say it, it would be done. And now, if the Lord has such great power, and has wrought so many miracles among the children of men, how is it that he cannot instruct me, that I should build a ship?[3].

These promises are for you as well. Take that last line and say, "How is it that he cannot instruct me, that I should [give a good talk]?"

Elder Bednar looks at Nephi as one who believes Christ; he puts it this way:

> I am acquainted with Church members who accept as true the doctrine and principles contained in the scriptures... and yet they have a hard time believing those gospel truths apply specifically in their lives and to their circumstances. They seem to have faith in the Savior, but they do not believe His promised blessings are available to them or can operate in their lives[4].

Nephi believed in those promises; he could turn water into land if God asked him to do it. We can have that same confidence if we are asked to serve. The promised blessings are available to us right now in our present-day circumstances.

Moroni is another example of believing Christ; when Moroni felt weak, he went to the Lord and received this promise that applies to each of us. The Lord said,

> My grace is sufficient for the meek... And if men come unto me I will show unto them their weakness. I give unto men weakness that they may be humble; and my grace is sufficient for all men that humble themselves before me; for if they humble themselves before me, and have faith in me, then will I make weak things become strong unto them[5].

The 2% Principle:

For my next talk I will _____

_____

_____

_____

_____

_____

_____

_____

_____

Small Summary	
-Ability can be achieved with Christ's grace-	
Avoid These Traps	Try These Tips
• *Anxiety should not be used as a way to get out of the talk* • *You look at the talk as a task to do rather than an opportunity to grow from* • *When finished you say to yourself, "I'm glad that's over with"*	• *You don't need to get rid of anxiety; it humbles you; ask for divine help* • *You come closer to Christ as you ask for His help* • *When finished say to yourself, "Now that I have done that, what else can I do with God's help?"*

33

References/Resources:

1. YouTube: A Discussion on Mental Health: Episode 1 – Steve Young

2. LDS Living, October 20, 2021, "How Steve Young believes anxiety helped him become the man he is today," Daniel K Judd

3. 1 Nephi 17:50-51

4. Ensign, November 2016, "If Ye Had Known Me," David A. Bednar

5. Ether 12:26-27

6. YouTube: Steve Young Gratifying Hall of Fame Speech

7. Friend Magazine, June 2014, Question Corner "I get really nervous whenever it's my turn to give a talk in church. What are some things I can do to not feel so scared next time?"

The Relationship Between Emotion and logic

"Most of our mistakes, the big ones at least,
are the result of allowing emotion to overrule logic.
We knew the right choice but didn't obey."
-Unknown

I had a friend who, on his first time at the pulpit as a new bishopric member, got his words mixed, said the wrong names, lost his place, and felt like he was a failure. He didn't believe he could do this calling for another five years. After the service, he told me, "I practiced all morning, I had everything written down, but when I got up there, I don't know what happened."

I asked him, "Did you practice controlling your emotions?" He asked me what I meant by that, so I explained that emotion and logic have a negative relationship—this does not mean they have a bad relationship. A negative relationship means when one goes up the other goes down, and it takes practice to find the balance.

In the days before your own talk, you may be as confident and as ready as my friend, but when the day comes, you stand at the podium, see all the eyes on you... and... you... blank...

As this Gary Larson, Far Side cartoon suggests, maybe we don't give Tarzan enough credit; maybe he was super intelligent, but he bumbled his words around Jane because he was smitten by her beauty.

Controlling emotions needs to be a proactive choice, and practicing control helps us respond to the situation instead of reacting to it. Positive self-talk and practicing relaxation are great ways to handle your emotions and are the most effective form of preparation. Let's divide the rest of this chapter into two sections:

Section 1. Pre-talk Prep
- Positive self-talk
- Practice Controlling Emotions
- Breathing Practice on the Stand

Section 2. During the Talk Tips
- One Slow Inhale
- Give Yourself Permission to Pause
- The Lord is With You

Section 1: Pre-talk Prep:

Positive Self-talk:

We all have negative self-talk; it is common and normal. Knowing how to talk back to ourselves is really a key life skill. Below is a chart and how to use it for public speaking, but you can use this for any situation in your life. I left some blank spaces so you can add your own.

Please note, this exercise does not get rid of anxiety; instead, it can help us view our situations better and soothe our anxieties so that we can keep moving forward.

My Negative Thought	My Rewrite
They will see me shaking	Let them see; I will tell the congregation that I am nervous, yet willing, and they will root for me, and support me
Someone else would be better at giving this talk	Only I can give my own perspective, maybe I think about this topic differently and someone will learn something new
I am going to look like a fool	I give patience to others, they will do the same to me
I didn't prepare enough	It's only a 10 minute talk and will go by faster than I think; I did my best and the Lord is with me
Everyone will think I am stupid	I can't read people's minds. I will do my best and believe any positive feedback I get from others. I can do this!

39

Practice Controlling Your Emotions:

Practicing your talk in front of a family member or a friend is a good way to prepare; this helps you learn how to balance that emotion and logic and respond well when that time comes. This practice is also a safer place where you can make mistakes and do things over if you need to. Take notes on the emotions that come up, the thoughts you have, and get used to those emotions so they don't distract you.

Breathing Practice on the Stand:

In an interview after hosting the game show Jeopardy, Aaron Rogers (quarterback for the Green Bay Packers) was asked if there were any pre-football game rituals that helped him handle being the host on TV. He spoke of a simple exercise he uses on the sidelines called box breathing, also known as square breathing[1].

Box breathing is something you can do on the stand before you go up and talk; it can be done very subtly so that no one in the audience will know you are using it. Simply inhale for a count of 4, hold for a count of 4, exhale for a count of 4, hold the exhale for a count of 4, and repeat.

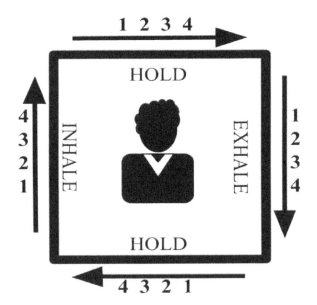

This practice actually helps to slow down the heart rate, calm the central nervous system, and soothe anxiety. If quarterbacks in very high-stakes games use this method to calm down, it can help us before our talks as well. In football, they use this breathing technique on the sidelines before going on the field. There are different tips to use when in the thick of the action.

Section 2: During the Talk Tips:

One Slow Inhale:

Square or box breathing is a good preparation exercise, but because of the time it takes, it is less practical in the middle of your talk. But one slow, calm inhale is all it takes to bring back the same effect. During your talk, if you lose your place or can't find a scripture, take one slow, calm inhale through your nose. This brings all the feelings that box breathing does into the moment and also gives you a timer; if you have not found the scripture or the thought by the time you need to exhale, then it is time to apologize and move on. It also helps that you can talk right away as you exhale, you don't need to take another breath and then speak. With practice it can be very fluid and subtle.

Give Yourself Permission to Pause:

I once was listening to a preacher who broadcasted out of Chicago on the radio. He was very energetic and had two members of his congregation in the booth with him, adding "amens" and "hallelujahs" while he spoke. I loved it! One time the preacher said, "Hold on while I find this verse," and one of the side members said, "Take your time," and I loved that too. This simply means when we ask the audience for time, they will give it to us. Before you take your one slow, calm inhale simply say, "Hold on while I find my place" and the audience will respond with an internal, "Take your time." So take your time, about as long as that one inhale.

The Lord is With You:

Please also remember, you do not have to do this alone. Practice, be ready, do your breathing, yet also reach out to the Lord for His power and grace, and He will soothe and strengthen you: "And it came to pass that the Lord did visit them with his Spirit, and said unto them: Be comforted. And they were comforted"[2].

41

The 2% Principle:

In my next talk or testimony I will _____

_____

_____

_____

_____

_____

_____

_____

Small Summary -Practice handling emotions, and give yourself permission to take your time-	
Avoid These Traps	Try These Tips
• Uncontrolled emotions make us feel like we weren't ourselves during the talk	• Control your emotions with intentional practice
• Uncontrolled emotions will make the decisions for us	• Square breathing on the stand, paced breathing at the microphone
• Uncontrolled emotions lead to nervous laughter, disclaimers, and distracting stories or topics	• One breath works to calm you when you are looking for a scripture or a quote, and as a timer to tell you when to move on if you don't find it.

References/Resources:

1. YouTube: Pregame Rituals '4:15' Jeopardy Interview
2. Alma 17:10

Magnify Your Assignment, but Keep It Simple

"Simplicity boils down to two steps:
Identify the essential. Eliminate the rest."
-Leo Babauta

Roger Bacon, a British philosopher, and mathematician during the Middle Ages, made impressive contributions to the studies of science and language. He took his studies and the research of others very seriously, in an attempt to help older scholars with failing eyesight continue their work, Roger Bacon was one of the first people ever mentioned to use a magnifying lens[1].

A magnifying lens is a convex shape that bulges outwards and is usually made of glass or plastic. As light hits the lens, it gets refracted, or bent, towards the center; as the light leaves the glass, it refracts even further. This means that if you hold up a glass in front of a leaf, you will see a larger image of the actual leaf in the lens. Through this process, the lens helps you to see the leaf in much greater detail than with your naked eye. You must remember one important fact: the size of the leaf itself did not change; but your ability to see greater detail improved.

When we attempt to magnify our callings or our assignment to speak, we do not need to make them bigger, grander, or more elaborate. We don't need to add more, make the task larger, or make it heavier. We must use faith, prayer, and revelation to magnify the understanding of the topic so we can address the right details that fit our ward family.

Elder Uchtdorf stated:

> Are we making our discipleship too complicated? …sometimes we take the beautiful lily of God's truth and gild it with layer upon layer of man-made good ideas, programs, and expectations… we need to make a conscientious effort to devote our energy and time to the things that truly matter while uplifting our fellowmen and building the kingdom of God[2].

As we prepare our talks, avoid making the assignment more complicated than it needs to be. Being allotted five or ten minutes for a talk does not give us much time, but as we pray for inspiration and focus on the members of our ward, we will find the right scriptures, the right quotes, and the right examples or stories to bring them hope, relief, and strengthen their testimonies

(See all of Part Three: Invite Revelation and Testify, and Part Four: Crafting Examples That Focus on the Message).

The 2% Principle:

For my next talk I will _____

_____

_____

_____

_____

_____

_____

_____

Small Summary -A conscientious effort to the things that truly matter-	
Avoid These Traps	Try These Tips
• *Get lost in the thick of thin things, the parts that don't matter*	• *Prayer, faith, and revelation to magnify the topic and see the right details*
• *Get lost in elaborate explanations and/or stories*	• *Stick to the basic points of your topic*
• *Lose the audience by telling jokes or the story of how you got asked to speak; these don't relate to your topic*	• *A short talk is memorable and more powerful than one with many different parts to it*

References/Resources:

1. First magnifying glass | Guinness World Records

2. Ensign, November 2015, "It Works Wonderfully!" Dieter F. Uchtdorf

3. See all of Part Three: Invite Revelation and Testify, and Part Four: Crafting Examples That Focus on the Message

4. Here is a trailer for NASA's going back to the moon. They pack a ton of information into a 3 minute and 47 second video because they only give the most important details (YouTube: NASA May 2019, "We Are Going"). Imagine giving a talk with this much information yet using less than four minutes of the meeting.

"...they had given themselves to much prayer, and fasting; therefore they had the spirit of prophecy, and the spirit of revelation, and when they taught, they taught with power and authority of God."
- Alma 17:3

"I urge all… who are called to speak in a meeting… we don't have to use soaring language or convey deep insights. Simple words of testimony will do. The Spirit will give you the words for you to speak and will carry them down into the hearts of humble people who look for truth from God. If we keep trying to speak for the Lord, we will be surprised someday to learn that we have warned, exhorted, taught, and invited with the help of the Spirit to bless lives, with power far beyond our own."
-Henry B Eyring

Part 3:
Invite Revelation and Testify

Refrain from Announcing Your Topic

"No sentence can be effective if it contains facts alone.
It must contain emotion, image, logic, and promise."
-Eugine M. Schwartz

A short story or a personal experience inspires listening more effectively and lets the congregation discover the topic on their own. Emotion, image, logic, and promise are how stories are created, they hook the reader to make the learning experience memorable. Elder David A. Bednar demonstrates this principle in his 2014 talk "Bear Up Their Burdens With Ease" by telling of a friend's truck being stuck in the snow; his friend continued the work of filling the truck bed with wood, and the load of wood is what helped the truck become unstuck. I am sure others were just as curious as to the gospel tie-in at the end of the brief story; Elder Bednar then stated the following: "Sometimes we mistakenly may believe that happiness is the absence of a load. But bearing a load is a necessary and essential part of the plan of happiness"[1]. This was not an announcement of the topic but an instructive statement that brought insight, clarity, and a more focused curiosity. This continues to be one of my favorite talks. The story and supporting scriptures help me apply the talk to my personal and professional life. Whenever I feel "stuck" my mind goes back to the story and I become grateful for my "load". The keyword "stuck" gives me an opportunity to look for strength from heaven and gain the traction to start moving again. This is the goal of a speaker: to influence your audience with practical insights they can apply to their lives.

As I use this principle in my own talks, it is interesting how people respond to what they have heard. One time I got comments like this:

- "I feel I understand how grace works better."
- "That helped me understand the Spirit better."
- "I now know why daily scripture study is important."

All these comments came after the exact same talk. By not directly announcing the topic, the Spirit guides their thoughts to what they need to hear and helps them consider the improvements they can make in their daily life, or to gain clarity on a gospel question. I am a believer that forgoing the announcement of our topics creates curiosity in the congregation and gives access to a powerful principle of personal revelation.

Elder Bednar identifies this principle as "hearing what is not said" and describes it as,

> The individual and personal thoughts, feelings, and impressions we receive by the power of the Holy Ghost are the things we are hearing that are not being said. Focusing primarily and exclusively on the content of a teacher's or speaker's message may in fact distract us from the impressions and answers God is sending to us by the power of His Spirit[2].

 Have you ever spoken to friends after a session of General Conference and mentioned you loved Elder or Sister so-and-so's talk on such-and-such? To only hear your friend say, "Was their talk on such-and-such? I thought they talked on this-and-that." This is the power of this principle of revelation. Announcing your topic isn't necessary, and sometimes it may distract the listener from "the impressions and answers God is sending [them]."

A scriptural insight, a question, a short story, or a personal example draws the congregation into your talk and creates curiosity for the audience to discover the topic on their own. You and the congregation will be amazed at the power of revelation that comes from this simple change.

The 2% Principle:

For my next talk I will _____

_____

_____

_____

_____

_____

_____

Small Summary -Create curiosity and draw the audience in-	
Avoid These Traps	Try These Tips
• *Avoid giving a factual statement on the topic just to fill time*	• *Give the congregation "emotion, image, logic, and promise" and inspire curiosity*
• *Avoid announcing the topic, as it can set their minds wandering, "another talk on…"*	• *Questions, short stories, and personal examples invite curiosity*
• *Avoid announcing the topic as it gives them only one topic to focus on*	• *Give the Spirit an opportunity to identify insights and questions people came to church for (the principle of "hearing what is not being said")*

References/Resources:

1. Ensign, May 2014, "Bear Up Their Burdens With Ease," David A. Bednar

2. Deseret Book, 2021, The Spirit of Revelation, David A. Bednar, p.17

Disclaimers Discredit You

*"Jesus Christ said
'by their fruits ye shall know them,'
not by their disclaimers."*
-William S. Burroughs

My twelve-year-old son, Jeffrey, was sitting on the stand in front of a large congregation waiting for his turn to speak. His legs were shaking, and he anxiously fidgeted with his fingers. As he got up and walked to the microphone, he held on tight to the pulpit with both hands. Standing up straight, he looked out to the congregation and took a deep breath. Without apology, he said with a small shake of his voice, "Brothers and sisters good morning. I'm really nervous today, and I ask for your faith to be added to mine as I express what I believe I should say." He continued, still shaking, "I am grateful for the opportunity I had this week to learn and grow. I want to share a few things from my study that have helped me come closer to Christ."

To the audience, it was a sudden transformation of a boy who was once nervous but now a confident speaker. The bishopric saw what was concealed from the congregation—a young man holding onto the pulpit for dear life. His legs were shaking like sewing machines for the duration of his talk. Yet, he did not start his talk with, "This is my first talk, so please bear with me," or, "I hope I do this OK. I was surprised the Bishop asked me to speak; I'll be quick." His exclamation of faith, especially when feeling vulnerable and insecure, was a powerful way to bring the Spirit into the service.

Avoiding disclaimers keeps the listener's attention on the intent of our talk and invested in our message. However, when we begin a talk with a disclaimer or an apology, we discredit our own witness and testimony. We are saying to the congregation that we aren't qualified to testify on the principles and doctrine of Jesus Christ. But we are qualified! President Thomas S. Monson taught, "Whom the Lord calls, the Lord qualifies"[1].

Imagine if the school crossing guard greeted you and your child with, "I'm not really the best person to do this. This is my first time and I hope I don't mess it up." This disclaimer would create a very awkward moment for you. We would rather hear an expression of faith or confidence like, "Alright kids, stick close, and follow me," rather than a disclaimer that only lowers our expatations and raises our anxiety.

When we offer a disclaimer, we are actually trying to soothe ourselves (See Part Two: The Relationship Between Emotion and Logic). We lack confidence, so we give a disclaimer to lower others' expectations in case we make a mistake. This is not an act of faith, but an act of doubt— doubt in yourself and in the Lord's ability to grant you His grace.

Here are some common disclaimers, you can add your own.

I'm not the best person for this.	I'll try not to take up too much time.
Well, those first talks were so good, we should just end the meeting right now.	I noticed the Bishop's phone number but decided to pick up anyway.
I tried to get out of this, but here it goes.	Ever had that temptation to call in sick? I had that this morning.
This is my first talk so I hope it works out.	I totally forgot I was speaking until last night.
Brother/Sister So-and-so would be better for this topic than me.	I didn't really prepare anything.

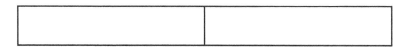

Enoch, Moses, and Jeremiah all had doubts about their ability to speak in public. We can learn from their example as we recognize a pattern in their interactions with God.

1.   The Call From The Lord

"…Enoch, my son, prophesy unto this people, and say unto them— Repent…"[3]

2.   Expression of Doubts to The Lord

"And Moses said unto the Lord, O my Lord, I am not eloquent… I am slow of speech, and of a slow tongue."[4]

3.   The Lord Promises His Help

"Be not afraid of their faces: for I am with thee to deliver thee, saith the Lord.
"Then the Lord put forth his hand, and touched my mouth. And the Lord said unto me, Behold, I have put my words in thy mouth."[5]

4.   Acting In Faith as The Lord Qualifies Them

"And so great was the faith of Enoch that he led the people of God… and he spake the word of the Lord, and the earth trembled, and the mountains fled… so great was the power of the language which God had given him."[6]

The following promise is still in force for you and me: "Treasure up in your minds continually the words of life, and it shall be given you in the very hour that portion that shall be meted unto every man"[7].

Elder Jeffrey R. Holland proclaimed,

I am not asking you to pretend to faith you do not have. I am asking you to be true to the faith you do have. Sometimes we act as if an honest declaration of doubt is a higher manifestation of moral courage than is an honest declaration of faith. It is not![8].

Imagine if Moses walked into the court of Egypt and said, "So ... um ... Pharaoh, I know I'm not the most well-spoken, and ... um ... I'm probably not the best person to ask, but... Will you let The Lord's people go?" What Moses actually said to Pharaoh was full of faith and confidence: "Thus saith the Lord God of Israel, Let my people go"[9].

Follow the pattern:
1. Be called... by the bishopric
2. Express your fears to the Lord in your prayers and preparation
3. Accept his promises and grace with faith in Jesus Christ
4. Act in faith, The Lord will provide a way for you to act in confidence.

Nephi knew this pattern and followed it with faith, he Said,

> I will go and do the things which the Lord hath commanded, for I know that the Lord giveth no commandments unto the children of men, save he shall prepare a way for them that they may accomplish the thing which he commandeth them[10].

The deep fear within each of us may not be what we expect. Notice the effect overcoming this fear has on others.

Our Deepest Fear:
Our deepest fear is not that we are inadequate.
Our deepest fear is that we are powerful beyond measure.
It is our light not our darkness that most frightens us.
We ask ourselves, who am I to be brilliant, gorgeous,
talented, and fabulous?
Actually, who are you not to be?
You are a child of God.
Your playing small does not serve the world.
There's nothing enlightened about shrinking so that other
people won't feel insecure around you.
We were born to make manifest the glory of
God that is within us.
It's not just in some of us; it's in everyone.
And as we let our own light shine,
we unconsciously give other people
permission to do the same.
As we are liberated from our own fear,
Our presence automatically liberates others.
*—**Marianne Williamson**[11]*

Whenever I hear, "I'm not the best person for this topic," my first thought is, "If you act in faith, control your emotions, and embrace some vulnerability, you may be the perfect person to teach us today." Walk up to that podium as a nervous, vulnerable, and living example of faith in Christ.

The 2% Principle:

In my next talk or Testimony I will _____

_____

_____

_____

_____

_____

_____

_____

Small Summary	
-A statement of faith is better than an expression of doubt-	
Avoid These Traps	Try These Tips
• *Disclaimers set the wrong tone and say, "Please lower your expectations for me."*	• *Set an example of faith in Christ, "I ask that your faith be joined with mine"*
• *Accomplish the task, and check the box but you don't learn from the experience*	• *Accept the call from the Lord, express your doubts to him, then accept his grace and support*
• *Disclaimers only soothe you, and inflame your doubts and negative self-talk*	• *Focus on the faith you do have, hold fast to the ground you have already won*

References/Resources:

1. April 1996, "Duty Calls," Thomas S. Monsoon

2. See Part Two: The Relationship Between Emotion and Logic

3. Moses 6:27

4. Exodus 4:10

5. Jeremiah 1:8-9

6. Moses 7:12-13

7. Doctrine and Covenants 84:85

8. Ensign May, 2013 "Lord I Believe" Elder Jeffrey R. Holland

9. Exodus 5:1

10. 1 Nephi 3:7

11. Marianne Williamson, 1996, "A Return to Love: Reflections on the Principles of A Course in Miracles"

`

Avoid Random Stories, Filler Words, and Sounds

"The right word may be effective,
but no word was ever as effective
as a rightly timed pause"
-Mark Twain

In college, I remember listening to a speaker nervously talk to a large audience. The topic and stories were random with no clear organization and the speech was peppered with many filler words (right, like, ya know?) and sounds (tongue clicks, nervous laughter, lip-smacking) to fill the empty spaces. The effect on one audience member, in particular, was interesting to me. At the time I was studying American Sign Language (ASL) so I sat with the hearing-impaired group. The interpreter eventually stopped signing and indicated that he would now only attempt to summarize the most important points. He explained to us that the random stories were jumbled and the filler words and sounds were so distracting that he could not translate effectively. Just like this interpreter who could no longer translate the physical messages, the Spirit can also struggle to translate spiritual truths and testimony to the congregation, when a talk is too disjointed and disorganized. (See Part Two: The Relationship Between Emotion and Logic and Part Four: Proactive Preparation).

Sometimes when giving a talk, we tell random stories so the audience will know where we got our ideas from. The audience only needs our ideas; random stories take us further from the topic rather than solidifying it (See Part Four: Crafting Examples That Focus on the Message).

Filler words take up the space that the audience uses to ponder our words, and filler sounds only distract the congregation.

As you are looking for your place and moving forward, pauses allow the congregation time to think and gather their thoughts. As the quote at the beginning of the chapter says, a rightly-timed pause is better than anything else. Therefore, build time into your talk for you and the congregation to think.

Here is a list of filler words and sounds that you may hear yourself or others use. This is not all-inclusive. I've left a few spaces for you to write your own.

Filler Words	*Sounds*
And... Ummm	Lip smack
So; so…yeah	Tongue click
Like	Nervous laughter, Haha
Ya know? Ya know what I mean?	Breathing into the microphone
Right?	Tapping fingers
OK… Great, So	

There is no need to apologize, fill in gaps, or get off-topic. Give the audience the space and time, and they will return the favor. (See Part One: Embracing Vulnerability)

A Small Word of Encouragement:

These filler sounds and random stories can sometimes be a difficult habit to break. Some of us may not even know we have been doing these things. For me, the filler words "umm" and "ya know?" were my regulars and it took some patient practice to overcome. To this day they still occasionally slip in. I just acknowledge they came, take a breath, slow down, and move on. Please be patient with yourself, give yourself some time, and ask a friend to give you feedback on how you are doing—particularly on what you are doing well.

The 2% Principle:

In my next talk or testimony I will _____

_____

_____

_____

_____

_____

_____

_____

Small Summary -Random stories only distract us from the topic, they do not solidify it-	
Avoid These Traps	Try These Tips
• *You give in to the feeling of needing to fill the space*	• *Use pauses to give the congregation time to think*
• *You give into the feeling of needing to justify your connections with a random story*	• *Use examples but hone them and write them into your talk*
• *Get through the talk as fast as you can, to get it over quickly*	• *Be patient with yourself and ask a friend to give you positive feedback on how you are doing*

Resources:

1. See Part Two: The Relationship Between Emotion and Logic and Part Four: Proactive Preparation

2. See Part Four: Crafting Examples That Focus on the Message

3. See Part One: Embracing Vulnerability

66

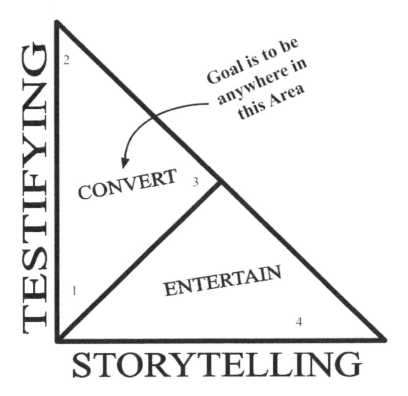

TESTIFYING

STORYTELLING

Goal is to be anywhere in this Area

CONVERT

ENTERTAIN

1. Simple Testimony
2. Direct and confident testimony
3. Testimony with a brief experience
4. Story with a brief testimony

Stories vs. Testimony

"Be sincere; be brief; be seated."
-Franklin D. Roosevelt

A legendary family story comes from a testimony meeting during my brother's mission. A woman came to the pulpit and spoke of her pet bird. It was a rare and exotic bird, a bird she had wanted to purchase for a long time. She saved money for the bird, purchased the bird, and when she got home, it was glorious for all to behold. The story went on and on, and her rhetoric was elegant, voluble, and loquacious. Her descriptions of everything bird-related were fanciful, flowery, and vibrant.

Then tragedy struck when the bird escaped its cage and flew through an open front door. In a panic, the neighbors were called, the troops gathered, animal control was on the scene, and the woman was beside herself in dread, despondency, and despair. "What else can we do?" she lamented to the sky. After a long time spent looking, the bird was miraculously located. As this ten-minute story ended, she turned from the microphone and sat down.

I imagine someone visiting that day, shocked that she did not bear her testimony, instead focusing on her lost bird. I imagine them saying to themselves, "Isn't this a religious meeting? How did that story fit into our worship?"

Now imagine if this woman would have come to the pulpit, paused as she looked out to the congregation, and simply stated, "This week our family had a situation where we lost our pet bird out the front door. We were unsure of what to do or how to find it. As we gathered together and said a prayer, the answer came and things were resolved quickly." And then in closing, she could have said, "I bear you my testimony that prayer is real and God will also answer you as you have faith in him."

Simple language and brief testimony are more powerful than a story more eloquently or fancifully given[1].

A testimony should be personal and to the point; it does not need lengthy background information or references to bring the Spirit into the hearts of your congregation. Two years into Brigham Young's relationship with church members, before he was baptized, he was still struggling to understand if the restoration of the Gospel was true; he stated the following to express how simplicity in testimony touched him:

> When I saw a man without eloquence, or talents for public speaking, who could only say, "I know, by the power of the Holy Ghost, that the Book of Mormon is true, that Joseph Smith is a Prophet of the Lord," the Holy Ghost proceeding from that individual illuminated my understanding, and light, glory, and immortality were before me[2].

The purpose of a testimony is to bring the spirit of truth into the service and to bring people to Christ. It should fill our talk from start to finish. Yet sometimes, the purpose of our testimony is to simply end the talk. What if the first line in your talk could be a part of your testimony? "Brothers and sisters I have a testimony of the gospel of Jesus Christ, I know God lives, that His Spirit is real, and I would like to share some thoughts of how I have experienced God's goodness and mercy in my life." When we declare our testimony and that we want to share our own experiences and study, people start to sit up and pay attention. Use your own conviction and testimony to strengthen the start, middle, and end of your talk. This strengthens you and your audience as you move along.

President Hinkley stated, "This thing which we call testimony is the great strength of the Church. It is the wellspring of faith and activity. It is difficult to explain. It is difficult to quantify… yet it is as real and powerful as any force on the earth"[3].

Do you only testify once at the end of your talk? Does your talk or testimony bring people to Christ, or does it inspire them to pull out their phones and search for images of rare exotic birds?

The 2% Principle:

In my next talk or testimony I will _____

_____

_____

_____

_____

_____

_____

_____

Small Summary	
-Simple language and brief testimony are more powerful than a story-	
Avoid These Traps	Try These Tips
• *Get lost in details and background information; there becomes nothing to testify about*	• *Use testimony throughout your talk. Start with your testimony and how Christ impacts your life*
• *Using your testimony only to end your talk*	• *Be personal and to the point so the Spirit can specifically testify of truth*

References/Resources:

1. See Part One: Intent
2. Teaching, No Greater Call, **Journal of Discourses, 1:88**
3. Ensign May 1998 "Testimony" President Gordon B. Hinckley

"If I went back to college again, I'd concentrate on two areas:
learning to write and to speak before an audience.
Nothing in life is more important than
the ability to communicate effectively."
-Gerald R. Ford

"A speaker should approach his preparation
not by what he wants to say,
but by what he wants to learn."
-Tod Stocker

"Think like a wise man
but communicate in the language of the people."
- William Butler Yeats

Part 4:
Getting Started
And Putting it
Together

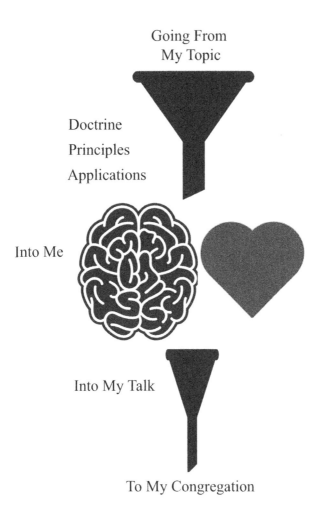

How to Prepare and Research in a Week

"There are three things to aim at in public speaking:
First, to get into your subject,
then to get your subject into yourself, and lastly,
to get your subject into the heart of your audience."
-Alexander Greg

A process I follow when I am asked to speak in the church has really helped me to be successful: I call it the "20/10/5 rule of preparation" and it works like a funnel—broad at the top and narrow at the bottom. Each part of the rule goes through the days of the week; I will give you the schedule and structure below. Let's say I got asked to speak on Sunday and I only had a week to prepare; this is how my process starts.

20: Sunday - Tuesday

I initially prepare as if I am guaranteed twenty minutes to give the talk. I think about the topic very broadly and I plan as if I have all day to give it and the audience is ready and willing to learn. This approach allows me to explore the big picture of the topic and also gives way to many applicable stories, examples, quotes, scriptures, and etc. It really helps me see the many different ways the talk could go.

This approach allows me to prayerfully examine the bible dictionary, read conference talks (and explore the references and sources for those conference talks), search the scriptures, comb through ensign articles, quiz my family, and browse hymn lyrics. This process takes an hour or more as I jot down ideas and let the Spirit guide me to personal applications of the topic. After this exercise I will use one or two trips to and from work (Monday and Tuesday), not listening to the radio or anything, just spouting off random thoughts and ideas pretending I am speaking to the congregation.

I specifically pray to know how the gospel principles apply to my life, since I want to use the most recent examples or experiences from that week in my talk. By Tuesday after work, I have a very long talk prepared. I now move to the next rule.

10: Wednesday and Thursday

Now I proceed as though I only have ten minutes to give my talk. Prayerfully, I start to cut the fluff, eliminating the unnecessary or time-consuming content that doesn't really contribute to the heart of the subject. I practice to and from work again and by Thursday I have a pretty good talk that I am proud of.

5: Friday and Saturday

What if the other speakers and the musical number go long? Now I only have five minutes to give my talk. After all the thoughts and preparation, now I need to narrow down the topic into its most important elements. I will only have room for one or two small examples that focus on the message[1] and hit the topic home. No time for jokes, disclaimers[2], or the story of how the bishop asked me to speak; I only have five minutes so it had better be engaging, to the point, and testify of Christ and His gospel. I will write down those parts I feel are the most important and practice that talk to-and-from work on Friday; with five minutes I can give the talk a few times before it get to work. Saturday morning I will spend a bit of time honing the topic and maybe try it out loud with one friend or my wife.

Sunday Morning

This is a time for reflection, a bit more prayer, and to ask God if there is anything else I could do and I ask for the Lord to be with me as I talk. The whole process helps to get the topic into my head and my heart, then onto paper, and then into the hearts of the congregation.

While I am on the stand doing my breathing exercises[3], I will listen to the talks and enjoy the service. I can then see how much time I have and write on the top of the page what time I need to be finished.

If I am given only seven minutes, then I may bring in that one story I wanted to tell but it was the third option. If I am given ten minutes, then I can also share the story and those two scripture examples I liked. If I only have five minutes, then I am ready to go with no problem.

This does bring up one last question: "What if, by my turn, I have the full twenty minutes left to give my talk?" Well, I look at it this way: I know that a good twelve-to-fifteen-minute talk is all that is needed to help the bishopric know they do not need to take any of the time; we can easily sing all the verses of the closing hymn and get out with two or three minutes to spare. How do you give a twelve-to-fifteen-minute talk? Simple, you give the fifteen-minute talk, add in one or two quotes or examples that got cut, and you talk a little bit slower.

The 2% Principle:

With my next talk or testimony _____

_____

_____

_____

_____

_____

Small Summary
-20,10,5 Rule: It's like a funnel, broad at the top, narrow at the bottom-

Avoid These Traps	Try These Tips
• *Struggle to make time in an already busy week, so you end up writing it on Saturday or Sunday Morning*	• *Use times in your week where you are not doing much to practice your talk: the drive to work, doing dishes, mowing the lawn, folding laundry, listening to music, going for a walk*
• *Instead of having a plan beforehand, you end up using your time on the stand to shorten your talk and decide your main topics*	• *Get into your subject: conference talks have tons of references for the topic (Bible Dictionary, Liahona Articles, Hymns, Scriptures)*
• *Use the only examples you can think of from your mission 20+ years ago*	• *Get your subject into yourself: show the Lord you want to do your best; he will lead you specifically to recent examples to use in your talk*

Resources:

1. See Part Four: Crafting Examples That Focus on the Message

2. See Part Three: Disclaimers Discredit You

3. See Part Two: The Relationship Between Emotion and Logic

4. "7 Tips for Giving a Talk" Sarah Hanson, Liahona July 2018

Outlining the Talk

*"If you can't explain it simply,
you don't understand it well enough."*
– Albert Einstein

Preparing a talk can be overwhelming, especially if you are unsure where to start. If you have felt this way, please know you are not alone. After you get up from your knees, asking Heaven for help, there are a few questions you can ask as you start your preparation: These questions start with why, where, what, and how?

"Why is this topic important?"

When we use the question "why," we can come closer to understanding the doctrine of the subject. As you ponder this question, the Spirit will give you some suggestions. As you search, ponder, and pray, your mind will try to answer this question and point out the doctrine.

"Where does this topic fit in the plan of salvation?"

Usually, our topics have to do with mortal life and helping us through it. This question helps put things into the eternal perspective. Does it go under a blessing, a trial, fulfillment of prophecy, tips of how to overcome, etc.?

"What are the most important points to understand with this topic?"

When we use the question of "what," we can identify the principles of this doctrine that help to define the way the topic fits into our lives.

"How can I, or do I, see this topic in my daily life?"

Elder Bednar's talk "We Believe In Being Chaste"[1] is a perfect example of how he uses why, where, what, and how in his outline. At the start, he asks the question, "Why is the law of chastity so important?" This allows the audience to ask the same question to themselves yet also states the doctrine he is focusing on. With each paragraph the doctrine is there, the principle is stated, and you can see the applications identified in each paragraph. Look at this table to identify the principles of outlining; then follow the link to read the full paragraphs in the talk.

Doctrine: Chastity "Why" question	"My message addresses a fundamental question of great spiritual consequence: Why is the law of chastity so important?"
Principles "Where" and What" Questions	Applications: "How" Questions
The Father's Plan of Happiness	The Father's plan enables His spirit sons and daughters to obtain physical bodies, to gain mortal experience, and to progress toward exaltation.
The Importance of a Physical Body	Our physical bodies make possible a breadth, a depth, and an intensity of experience that simply could not be obtained in our premortal existence.
The Power of Procreation	The power of procreation is spiritually significant. How we feel about and use that supernal power will determine in large measure our happiness in mortality and our destiny in eternity.
The Standard of Sexual Morality	The Church of Jesus Christ of Latter-day Saints has a single, undeviating standard of sexual morality: intimate relations are proper only between a man and a woman in the marriage relationship prescribed in God's plan.

The Natural Man	The precise nature of the test of mortality, then, can be summarized in the following question: Will I respond to the inclinations of the natural man, or will I yield to the enticings of the Holy Spirit and put off the natural man and become a saint through the Atonement of Christ the Lord (see Mosiah 3:19)? That is the test.
The Intent of the Adversary	Because a physical body is so central to the Father's plan of happiness and our spiritual development, Lucifer seeks to frustrate our progression by tempting us to use our bodies improperly. The very tool he does not have is thus the primary target of his attempts to lure us to spiritual destruction.
The Blessings of Being Chaste	Alma counseled his son Shiblon to "bridle all [of his] passions, that [he] may be filled with love" We also are promised that, as we pursue the pathway of virtue, "the Holy Ghost shall be [our] constant companion"
The Principle of Repentance	The results of sincere repentance are peace of conscience, comfort, and spiritual healing and renewal. Your bishop or branch president is the spiritual physician's assistant who is authorized to help you repent and heal.
A Promise and a Testimony	The doctrine I have described will seem to be archaic and outdated to many people in a world that increasingly mocks the sanctity of procreation and minimizes the worth of human life. Chastity and virtue are now, always have been, and always will be "most dear and precious above all things" (Moroni 9:9). I so testify…

Another example:

On the following page is my outline for the next chapter of this book. I'll show you how I broke the topic down into principles and then you can read the final product (applications) in the next few pages[2].

Outline	Principles
Title (intent of the chapter)	***Crafting Examples That Focus on the Message***
Personal example that is short and to the point to gain interest	A life-changing moment playing basketball with my friend Jac
Tie in the story to the topic	Our own examples need to be like Jac's statement and my example: short, to the point, and focused on the message.
Explain the trap/topic	If we don't craft our personal examples we can struggle to tell the story and the congregation can get lost in unnecessary details
Show a good example	Elder Maxwell's talk where he gives well-crafted examples "Remember How Merciful the Lord Hath Been"[3]
Identify the principles	Show the principles in each example of how he focused on the message
Testify	Restate a summary of the point

There are a number of ways to craft your talk and give your thoughts, examples, and testimony. As you study the apostle you like most, ask the opinion of a friend, or use the outlines in this book, you will find your own style. As you practice, you will find what works for you and be able to write a well-organized talk very quickly[4].

The 2% Principle:

With my next talk or testimony _____

_____

_____

_____

_____

84

Small Summary -If you can't explain it simply, you don't understand it well enough-	
Avoid These Traps	Try These Tips
• *Speaking simply of the concept in your head is a breeding ground for randomness*	• *Asking the right questions helps to focus and organize your topic: why, where, what, how?*
• *Simply writing "Talk about _____ here," in your outline can derail your talk with unneeded details*	• *Doctrine goes throughout; each principle is each paragraph's topic, and the applications fill the paragraph*

References/Resources:

1. Ensign, May 2013, "We Believe In Being Chaste" David A Bednar

2. See Part Four: Crafting Examples that Focus on the Message

3. Ensign, May 2004 "Remember How Merciful the Lord Hath Been" Neil A Maxwell

4. See Part Four: Proactive Preparation

5. An example: Study how Elder Kelly crafted this article Come Follow Me, March 2022 "The Lord Was with Joseph," Elder Kelly R. Johnson

Crafting Examples That Focus on the Message

"When you talk, you don't think about what you are doing,
you just talk. But when you are a comedian
you have to analyze every aspect about how you communicate
and try to improve it."
-Jerry Seinfeld

I have always enjoyed playing basketball, and one particular night we had three teams competing, so one team rested while two teams played—the losing team sat while the winning team stayed on the court. As my team rested, I watched the star player on the winning team score at will and put the game away. I went to get a drink but came back too late to select who I wanted to defend, and I was left defending the star. I exclaimed in sarcasm, "Sure, make me guard the good guy!" My friend Jac leaned over to me and simply stated, "You're good too." For some reason this simple statement had an effect on me; it led me to keep that star scoreless for the next game and followed me into my career and my role as a father. Jac did not give background information about this statement; he did not try to convince me through famous quotes or motivational storytelling. His one intent was to convey his confidence in me, and I got the message.

During a talk, we have opportunities to use our own personal experience to highlight the principle or solidify the message, yet we sometimes believe background information, famous quotes, or motivational storytelling are the needed tools. In the end, all that is needed is a true intent to convey our confidence in our message.

The trap of getting lost in the details is especially dangerous if we are reminded of a random story during our talk or if we leave our example to a simple sentence in our outline saying, "Tell the story about _____ here." If we are not prepared to tell the story, then we can get lost in it and accidentally leave the intended message on the back burner instead of in the forefront of the congregation's minds.

Elder Neil A. Maxwell demonstrates this principle masterfully in his April 2004 talk, "Remember How Merciful the Lord Hath Been"[1]. In this talk he tells twelve stories of different life lessons and gospel principles in less than fifteen minutes; it is a masterpiece of focusing on the message. Here are three of his examples we can use as blueprints for sharing our own life experiences:

> …My sister Lois, legally blind from birth, not only coped but served well as a public school teacher for 33 years. She had that same reflex possessed by those pioneer souls who quietly picked up their handcarts and headed west, a reflex we all need. So if various trials are allotted to you, partake of life's bitter cups, but without becoming bitter.

> Soon after arriving home from World War II, I had promises to keep (Robert Frost, "Stopping by Woods on a Snowy Evening," in The Poetry of Robert Frost, ed. Edward Connery Lathem [1969], 225)—meaning going on a mission now. I grew tired of waiting for the bishop. And in some early ark-steadying, I went to the bishop's home and said I had saved the money and wanted to go, so let's "get this show on the road." The good bishop hesitated, and then said he'd been meaning to ask me about going.

> Years later, I would learn from that bishop's devoted ward clerk that the bishop had felt I needed a little more time with my family after having been away so far and for a tenth of my life. Hearing this, I chastised myself for having been too judgmental. (See Bruce C. Hafen, A Disciple's Life: The Biography of Neal A. Maxwell [2002], 129–30.)

> No wonder the wise father of Elder Henry B. Eyring observed once how the Lord had a perfect Church until He let all of us inside!...

> Having virtually no quantitative skills, I was seldom if ever able to help our children with math and scientific subjects. One day our high school daughter Nancy asked me for "a little help" regarding a Supreme Court case, Fletcher v. Peck. I was so eager to help after so many times of not being able to help. At last a chance to unload! Out came what I knew about Fletcher v. Peck. Finally my frustrated daughter said, "Dad,

I need only a little help!" I was meeting my own needs rather than giving her "a little help." We worship a Lord who teaches us precept by precept, brethren, so even when we are teaching our children the gospel, let's not dump the whole load of hay[1].

Elder Maxwell did not give any more details about his sister than was needed: We know she was blind, a tough soul, and not bitter. The message? We should be the same. He told no war stories or mission stories, only one personal story. The message? Don't be too judgemental, and never believe we are perfect. He didn't give details about his learning issues or struggles in school, yet we know he had them, and he wanted to help his children. The message? We should focus on our children's needs first and help as a loving Lord helps.

As the quote at the top of this segment says, don't just talk, "analyze every aspect about how you communicate and try to improve it." A well-crafted example that is focused on the right details leaves a lasting memory the Spirit can sink into the hearts and minds of those who hear it.

The 2% Principle:

With my next talk or testimony _____

_____

_____

_____

_____

_____

Small Summary	
-Analyze every aspect about how you communicate-	
Avoid These Traps	Try These Tips
• *Belief that background information, famous quotes, or motivational storytelling are the needed tools to convert* • *Focusing more on story rather than a message*	• *A well-crafted example helps the Spirit sink the message into the audience's hearts.* • *A true intent helps convey your confidence in your message and invites pondering*

References/Resources:

1. Ensign May 2004 "Remember How Merciful the Lord Hath Been" Neil A Maxwell

Proactive Preparation

"It usually takes me more than three weeks
to prepare a good impromptu speech."
-Mark Twain

I had a companion on my mission that read twenty pages in the Book of Mormon every day so he could read the Book of Mormon once a month for his whole mission. That was amazing to witness, and I could not believe the insights and teaching ability he had. I remember him being asked to speak spontaneously a number of times in church, and each time he would just sit on the stand and do nothing to show any sign of preparation; he would sit and listen to the service; he never had his scriptures out, never wrote any notes. Every time it was the same thing: He would walk up to the pulpit, open his scriptures and say, "This morning when I was reading in the Book of Mormon…" and then he would give a five-to-fifteen-minute talk and testimony on the insights he learned from his daily studies. Because he was always prepared ahead of time, he enjoyed sharing his insights, and his audience enjoyed them too.

Reading twenty pages a day fit his style and personality; we don't have to do the same. However, we do need to find our own style of study and be consistent with it. Some people love to study in the morning; some do it at night; some in the car (audio); and some watch conference videos or listen to talks while they get ready for the day. I know a friend that watches the video in the shower. Find what works for you. As you do your best to put the word into your heart and mind, you will have the Spirit with you. When you are asked to speak in church, the Spirit will come as Jesus promised, "But the Comforter, which is the Holy Ghost... he shall... bring all things to your remembrance, whatsoever I have said unto you"[1].

When you receive a topic by the bishopric, ideas may come to your mind from the Spirit on what to say. You might also have other inspirations and ask the Bishop, "Do you mind if I speak on _____? I have been studying that topic lately." Often, the Bishop will agree. Sometimes he won't. Either way, take comfort in the Lord's promise, "Neither take ye thought beforehand what ye shall say, but treasure up in your minds continually the words of life, and it shall be given you in the very hour that portion that shall be meted unto every man"[2].

Very often you may be given a topic by the Bishop that you haven't been studying personally at the moment. However, with proactive preparation, as you reflect on many concepts, you will learn how to tie in the assigned topic to the principles that you have been studying or pondering, and this is how you develop your references and examples.

For instance, if you have been studying the plan of salvation and are asked to speak on prophets, you speak about how prophets are part of the plan. Or you have been studying church history, the life of the pioneers, or Joseph Smith and are asked to speak on the life of Christ. You can bring in examples from those early saints as they learned of Christ, or how they tried to be more Christ-like. A favorite story I would use to tie in early saints and the life of Christ is when Joseph Smith was criticized for doing women's work by "taking care of the children and the domestic chores" Joseph set the men straight by saying, "Go and do likewise" a quote from Christ in the New Testament, the story of the good Samaritan[3].

As we search, ponder, and pray, the Spirit will give us the same promise as Hyrum Smith. Hyrum had great intent to preach the gospel, yet the Lord gave him [and us] great council: "Seek not to declare my word, but first seek to obtain my word, and then shall your tongue be loosed; then, if you desire, you shall have my Spirit and my word, yea, the power of God unto the convincing of men"[4].

94

The 2% Principle:

With my next talk or testimony _____

_____

_____

_____

_____

_____

Small Summary *-His Spirit + His word = the power of God unto the convincing of men-*	
Avoid These Traps	Try These Tips
• *Only study when it's time to speak* • *You believe daily scripture study means sitting at a desk and being a scriptorian* • *Believe you don't have time*	• *Find your own personal, daily, spiritual fill, no matter the amount* • *The Holy Ghost will bring back memories from months ago, which will help with your talk* • *Believe you can make time*

References/Resources:

1. John 14:26

2. Doctrine and Covenants 84:85

3. Luke 10:37; Joseph Smith Lecture 2: Joseph's Personality and Character | BYU Speeches, Truman G Madsen

4. Doctrine and Covenants 11:21

5. "Speaking in Church" From the Life of President Heber J Grant

"You adapt. You overcome. You improvise."
-Clint Eastwood

"We cannot direct the wind,
but we can adjust the sails"
-Dolly Parton

Part 5:
Adapt To Other Occourrences

Speaking from an
Assigned Conference Talk

"If you steal from one author it's plagiarism;
if you steal from many it's research"
-Wilson Mizner

A talk on someone else's talk—for the speaker and the congregation—can sound like receiving a memo from the department of redundancy department. As the one who is assigned the talk, we can feel we are not going to speak in a way that is as sharp as the original talk. We can feel overwhelmed and insecure, and this easily leads to a tempting disclaimer: "They gave this talk way better than I could so I suggest you go read the talk" (See Part Three: Disclaimers Discredit You)[1]; this temptation needs to be resisted. The bishopric actually didn't assign you to talk on the talk; they want you to emphasize the doctrine and principles taught and to present them in a way that applies to your life and to the congregation.

Here are a three tips you can use to enhance the congregation's understanding of the topic while using your own style and the strength of your testimony:

1: Don't tell them what you are doing; you don't need to let the congregation know you are speaking from a conference talk—just have it be the source of your quotes and scriptures, and convey the overall message of the talk in your own way. Their talk should support your talk, not be your talk (See Part Three: Refrain from Announcing Your Topic)[2].

2: Break the talk down into the doctrine and the principles the original author is teaching, and let that study help inspire the direction your talk should go (See Part Four: Outlining the Talk)[3].

My daughter Emma, in her young single adult ward, received an assignment to speak on the 2021 conference talk "One Percent Better" by Elder Michael A. Dunn[4]. This is how she broke it down on a document.

Doctrine "Why?"	Principles "What?"
"Be ye therefore perfect" Eternal-Progression	"What if we applied that same principle to the very sweet and savory second principle of the gospel, repentance?"
"Come unto Christ and be perfected in him"	"Instead of trying to perfect everything, what if we tackled just one thing?"
And so it is with our Savior, who, though sinless, "received not of the fulness at first, but continued from grace to grace, until he received a fulness."	Could aggregating small but steady marginal gains in our lives finally be the way to victory over even the most pesky of our personal shortcomings? Can this bite-sized approach to tackling our blemishes really work?
Repentance is not an event; it is a process. It is the key to happiness and peace of mind. When coupled with faith, repentance opens our access to the power of the Atonement of Jesus Christ."	"If you can get just one percent better at something each day, by the end of a year … you will be 37 times better."
For behold, thus saith the Lord God: I will give unto the children of men line upon line, precept upon precept, here a little and there a little;	I know that it can sometimes feel like 1 percent forward and 2 percent back. Yet if we remain undaunted in our determination to consistently eke out those 1 percent gains, He who has "carried our sorrows" will surely carry us.
"Preparing to walk guiltless before God is one of the primary purposes of mortality and the pursuit of a lifetime; it does not result from sporadic spurts of intense spiritual activity."	"Small, steady, incremental spiritual improvements are the steps the Lord would have us take."

She then summarized the entire talk with this sentence:

> The focused doctrine is eternal progression through the principles of change/repentance line upon line, precept upon precept, through the applications of daily 1% goals that can help us to be more Christlike in the long run.

As she put her talk together, the examples became her own. She used some scriptures and quotes from the talk sparingly yet added other quotes and scriptures that came to mind during her preparation. As the quote at the top of the chapter says, "If you steal from one author it's plagiarism; if you steal from many it's research."

3: Apply the principles of their talk by sharing personal examples from your life; this makes the talk yours. Here is a small example from a section of my son's talk he gave during his senior year of high school. This is the end of the talk:

> In his talk from the last conference, Elder Dale G. Renlund spoke about how the people of the Democratic Republic of the Congo used to worship idols before they were converted to Christianity. Once they were converted they threw their idols into the churning waters of a waterfall. Elder Renlund states, "Being 'converted unto the Lord' means leaving one course of action, directed by an old belief system, and adopting a new one based on faith in Heavenly Father's plan and in Jesus Christ and His Atonement"[5].

> One way that this applied to my life was in my running career through my high school years. I ran on the cross country team for my school and I also I used to play pick-up basketball for fun. After having multiple basketball injuries that forced me to sit out entire seasons of cross country, I decided last year that—in order to stay healthy and become the best I can be—I needed to throw basketball into the waterfall. Through giving up basketball and keeping myself out of harm's way, I was able to have the best season of my career and really got myself to the level of competition that I always had the potential to be. This was made possible by me going all-in with running and putting aside the things that were holding me back.

> We can use this same level of commitment as we give up old habits or repent from sins that hold us back or put us in harm's way. I loved basketball, yet I loved cross country more. When I was all-in, my level of running improved dramatically. When we are converted and repent from our sins, when we are all-in, when we love Christ more than our

101

habits, our lives will improve just as dramatically.

Speaking from a conference talk is no different than writing any other talk; just use the study, inspiration, and quotes from the talk assigned. You may use the one talk as your main source of inspiration and focus, yet you can still use other quotes, scriptures, and personal examples to convey the doctrines taught. Make it your talk!

The 2% Principle:

Next time I am assigned a conference talk I will _____

_____

_____

_____

_____

_____

Small Summary
-No different than writing any other talk that uses quotes from conference talks-

Avoid These Traps	Try These Tips
• *Announcing the talk you are speaking from inspires them to pull out the talk on their phone*	• *Break the talk into doctrines and principles of the gospel and use your own personal examples of how you apply them to your life.*
• *Low confidence makes you try to give their talk instead of your own*	• *Give your thoughts, emotions, and the applications in your life since reading the talk*
• *Trying to give a talk on a talk is as redundant as redundancy*	• *Speak on the message of the talk, not the talk itself*

References/Resources:

1. See Part Three: Disclaimers Discredit You

2. See Part Three: Refrain from Announcing Your Topic

3. See Part Four: Outlining the Talk

4. Ensign, November 2021, "One Percent Better," Michael A. Dunn

5. Ensign, November 2019, "Unwavering Commitment to Jesus Christ," Elder Dale G. Renlund

Advice for
High Councilors

*"Always make a total effort,
even when the odds are against you."*
-Arnold Palmer

The best high councilor talks have a number of similar principles that make them successful. Let's go over them with a little bit of detail, and then you can add your own 2% more or less to make the talk different from other members of the Stake High Council (See Part One: Change The Script - The 2% Principle)[1].

They Seek Inspiration and Council:

You may not know the people in the congregation, and they may not know you. Put in some work beforehand that helps you mix the message the stake president wants you to give with the needs of the ward are. Seek council with the bishop about that mixture.

They Own It—Even the Bad Reputation of
Past High Councilors:

Understand and own that a congregation can be turned off to the possibility of a "dry-councilman" talk, and do not let that bother your preparation. Come in with confidence, purpose, and the love of the stake presidency (See Part Three: Invite Revelation and Testify)[2].

They Are to the Point:

I can't stress this enough: Don't begin your talk by naming your acquaintances from the pulpit in an attempt to demonstrate your familiarity with the ward. It will invite those few to perk up, but others to tune out. Say hello to the whole congregation, praise the speakers that came before you, and move on.

They Use a Short and Personal Experience in the Introduction:

Each congregation will give you at least 30 seconds of time to see what kind of talk this will be, so no disclaimers, no announcing of the topic, just start. Short and personal stories are what make the talk memorable, keep the congregation's attention, help tie in the topic, and leave an impression. A few years ago I had a high council speaker start right into a situation where his son had a huge hit on him while playing football; the boy lay on the ground for a few minutes and then ended up playing the rest of the game. As a parent, he was very worried about his boy, and later that night, when his son struggled with fatigue and concentration, they thought the big hit was the main issue, so they took him straight to the emergency room. Turned out his son was just dehydrated and needed fluids. This short, personal example helped him teach the principle of daily maintenance in spiritual things just like drinking water is a simple thing to do each day. The hit was not as bad as it looked, but a dehydrated person took longer to recover from it. This story kept my attention and helped me check if I was spiritually dehydrated. (See Part Four: Crafting Examples That Focus on the Message)[3].

They are Masters of the Accordion and Rulers of Time:

A good friend of mine who served on the high council for years once told me, "I don't know how to play the accordion but I learned a lot about how to stretch out my talk or condense it to fit the meeting." Becoming a master at managing time is a crucial part of being a positive contributor to the worship service (See Part Four: How to Prepare and Research in a Week; Part Five: Reducing Your Talk When Time Is Short)[4].

Share the love of the stake presidency in your testimony unless it helps in your introduction to your message (See Part Three: Refrain From Announcing Your Topic)[5].

The 2% Principle:

Next time I speak I will _____

_____

_____

_____

_____

_____

Small Summary
-No different than writing any other talk that uses quotes from conference talks-

Avoid These Traps	Try These Tips
• *Satisfied being as predictable or long-winded as other councilmen*	• *Seek inspiration from the Lord, and seek council from the bishop of what is needed*
• *Discredit yourself with disclaimers*	• *A short and personal experience In the introduction to introduce your topic*
• *Tell random stories to kill time*	• *Master the accordion: know how to shorten or lengthen your talk when needed*

Resources:

1. Part One: Change The Script - The 2% Principle

2. Part Three: Invite Revelation and Testify

3. Part Four: Crafting Examples That Focus on the Message

4. Part Four: How to Prepare and Research in a Week; Part Five: Reducing Your Talk When Time Is Short

5. Part Three: Refrain From Announcing Your Topic

6. Part Five: Speaking from a Conference Talk

7. Part Three: Stories vs. Testimony

Be Aware of Vulnerable Populations and Sensitive Topics

"Until you make the unconscious conscious,
it will direct your life..."
-Carl Jung

The plan of salvation works and is designed for all of God's children. God knows how to individualize the plan to each of his children so that in the end we will each "acknowledge… that all his judgments are just; that he is just in all his works, and that he is merciful unto the children of men"[1]. When we are asked to speak from the pulpit, we must abandon our own judgment and be inclusive to all of God's children. The more aware you are of those around you, the easier it is for the Spirit to advise you on how to apply your words to your congregation as you write your talk.

The Old Testament gives us a warning and great counsel: "A soft answer turneth away wrath: but grievous words stir up anger. The tongue of the wise useth knowledge aright: but the mouth of fools poureth out foolishness"[2]. Our talks need to be full of soft answers that are well-thought-out and researched with knowledge aright, with the intent to be inclusive and respectful. Yet we often pour out foolishness if we don't prepare well or don't ask for inspiration on how to be applicable to our whole congregation. Nephi reminded us how God views all of us, and we must do the same: "[The Lord God] denieth none that come unto him, black and white, bond and free, male and female; and he remembereth the heathen; and all are alike unto God, both Jew and Gentile"[3].

Here are three ways we can bring foolishness, but I also include ways to speak with the tongue of the wise:

1. Avoid comparing ourselves to other churches. As members of the Church, we don't like it when we hear others say, "you guys believe_____" However, I hear this same statement in talks, lessons, and conversations from members of the Church of Jesus Christ saying, "other churches believe_____". We must be as patient and kind to others as we want them to be to us; we must speak with a soft answer and the tongue of the wise.

2. Do your best to include those that don't believe they fit the mold of a member of the church, have different circumstances, or believe differently. To better understand what others are going through in their lives and to have knowledge aright see the page *Life Help*[4] on the Church's Gospel Library app or on their website. This site has tips for members and leaders on many different topics, and we can hear stories from those who struggle with these issues. We can learn how to be aware and even help. The more aware you are, with knowledge aright, the easier it is for the Spirit to advise you on how to apply the tongue of the wise to your congregation.

3. Avoid Politics. The Church is politically neutral and has offered this statement:

> The Church's mission is to preach the gospel of Jesus Christ... The Church of Jesus Christ of Latter-day Saints is neutral in matters of party politics. This applies in all of the many nations in which it is established... In the United States, where nearly half of the world's Latter-day Saints live, it is customary for the Church at each national election... emphasizing the Church's neutrality in partisan political matters.

> The Church does "reserve the right as an institution to address, in a nonpartisan way, issues that it believes have significant community or moral consequences or that directly affect the interests of the Church"[5].

Politics can be divisive and are not needed in our sacrament services. We must let the Church speak for itself in these matters, and we can focus our message on the Savior and his gospel.

Jesus Christ himself gave this instruction to the Nephites as He established His church among them, and it still holds true today:

And behold, ye shall meet together oft; and ye shall not forbid any man from coming unto you when ye shall meet together, but suffer them that they may come unto you and forbid them not; But ye shall pray for them, and shall not cast them out; and if it so be that they come unto you oft ye shall pray for them unto the Father, in my name[6]

He then reminds us how to act, like Him:

Therefore, hold up your light that it may shine unto the world. Behold I am the light which ye shall hold up—that which ye have seen me do... And ye see that I have commanded that none of you should go away, but rather have commanded that ye should come unto me, that ye might feel and see; even so shall ye do unto the world; and whosoever breaketh this commandment suffereth himself to be led into temptation[7]

To effectively communicate with each other, we must first realize that we are all different in the way we perceive the world. With a desire for personal connections, education, patience, charity, and the whisperings of The Spirit, we can use this understanding to guide our communication. The goal of every ward is to live in unity like those described in 4th Nephi:

The people were all converted unto the Lord... and there were no contentions and disputations among them, and every man did deal justly one with another. And they had all things common among them; therefore there were not rich and poor, bond and free, but they were all made free, and partakers of the heavenly gift... And there were great and marvelous works wrought... and in nothing did they work miracles save it were in the name of Jesus[8]

The 2% Principle:

Next time I prepare a talk bare my testimony I will _____

_____

_____

_____

_____

_____

Small Summary	
-A soft answer turneth away wrath… the tongue of the wise useth knowledge aright-	
Avoid These Traps	Try These Tips
• *Assume you know what is going on and end up speaking to those that fit the mold* • *You talk about other churches beliefs and bring in your own politics to the talk*	• *Study things out before you speak (Life Help Gospel Library app)* • *Seek kindness, inclusion, and respect*

References/Resources:

1. Alma 12:15

2. Proverbs 15:1-2

3. 2 Nephi 26:33

4. Life Help Gospel Library app

5. The LDS Church Believes in Political Neutrality

6. 3 Nephi 18:22-23

7. 3 Nephi 18:24-25

8. 4 Nephi 1:2-3

9. Resources on LGBTQ and Latter-Day Saint relationships and desire for unity: Official Website of the Church of Jesus Christ of Latter-day Saints on Same-Sex Attraction - kindness, inclusion, and respect

10. Non-Official Latter-day Saint LGBTQ Resource Center, "Introductory Articles"

Reducing Your Talk
When Time Is Short

"I've learned that people will forget what you said,
people will forget what you did,
but people will never forget how you made them feel."
-Maya Angelou

When we look at how long our talk is and compare it to how short the time is, we have to go back to the intent of our talk and what is most important at this moment. Elder Dallin H Oaks speaks about the sacrament being the most important item of the service; therefore, "Its content in addition to the sacrament should always be planned and presented to focus our attention on the Atonement and teachings of the Lord Jesus Christ,"[1]. Our intent must be on the sacrament and the Savior; if those two things have been focused on, then we can always save our talk for another time.

On the next page, I have a chart with a few options you can choose from when time is short; you may have others come to mind as well.

Overtime	If the bishop asks you to go overtime, then "…Behold, to obey is better than sacrifice"[2].
2 minutes left	Bear a small and simple testimony that goes along with the principles of the talks given before you. Ask the bishop if you can give your talk at a later date
5 minutes or less	Once you get up to the mic, tell people you are aware of the time and will not go over—this helps them relax and listen. "Brothers and sisters, I know I only have five minutes left, and I will not be able to give my full talk; let me leave one nugget of wisdom with you, and then I will close."
7 minutes or less	Give your introduction to identify the principle, share the best example from your talk, then bear testimony of the principle and Christ. If your planned talk is only 5-7 minutes long, then go for it.
10 minutes or less	Give your whole talk (if you know the time) or 70% of it; pick the best items that testify of Christ and teach the assigned principle.

In 2017 President Monson actually gave a three-minute talk on the blessings of having a testimony of the Book of Mormon. That talk was very impactful, but what I remember most was his testimony. He simply summarizes the other paragraphs of his talk in a beautiful way:

> My dear associates in the work of the Lord, I implore each of us to prayerfully study and ponder the Book of Mormon each day. As we do so, we will be in a position to hear the voice of the Spirit, to resist temptation, to overcome doubt and fear, and to receive heaven's help in our lives. I so testify with all my heart in the name of Jesus Christ, amen[3].

Inviting the Spirit through testimony can revive your audience; letting them know you are not going to go overtime also brings relief as some are worried about how much time they will have for their responsibilities in the next hour of church[4].

The 2% Principle:

Next I give a talk, if time is short, I will _____

_____

_____

_____

_____

_____

Small Summary *-People will remember how you made them feel-*	
Avoid These Traps	Try These Tips
• *Focus on your hard work and effort rather than the time and the effort of other teachers in the next hour* • *Give your talk as fast as you can* • *You forget to keep track of the time while everyone else is*	• *Focus on Christ and support the Sacrament (it's the purpose of the meeting)* • *Support the other talks and testify* • *Three-minute talks are possible with the right preparation*

References/Resources:

1. Ensign, November 2008, "Sacrament Meeting and the Sacrament," Elder Dallin H. Oaks

2. 1 Samuel 15:22

3. Ensign, May 2017, "The Power of the Book of Mormon," Thomas S Monson

4. See Part One: God Uses the Weak and Simple of the Earth

"Knowledge speaks, but wisdom listens."
- Jimi Hendrix

"My brothers and sisters,
it is now my assignment to speak to you,
and your assignment is to listen.
My goal is to finish my assignment before you finish yours."
- M. Russel Ballard

Part 6:
Being a Good
Participant

More Opportunities to Listen Than to Speak

*"Human beings, who are almost unique in
having the ability to learn from the experience of others,
are also remarkable for their apparent disinclination to do so."*
-Douglas Adams

A friend told me of a lesson he learned as a boy from his father. While sitting on a sacrament pew listening to the prelude music he thought he could smell cigarette smoke, but he wasn't sure. This filled him with anxiety because, as a young boy's limited understanding put it, someone was breaking a commandment and also coming to church. He asked his dad if that was smoke and his dad gave a profound answer: He said, "I love the smell of cigarettes in church because it means someone is trying."

As we sit in church and hear people struggle in their talks, we should try to cultivate the assumption that every speaker in our ward or branches is trying, since we all still need to improve. We must remember that we will always have more opportunities to listen to talks than to give them, so listening must be the skill we practice the most.

Henry Eyring, the father of President Henry B. Eyring, set the example for his son by talking to and asking questions of anyone that was around him. At one point, as a young boy, President Eyring asked his father, "Why do you ask gas station attendants questions?" His father's response was just as profound as my friend's father; he said, "I never met a man I couldn't learn something from"[1].

This is the great mindset we need to take into our gas stations and our sacrament services, to always believe we can learn something from whoever is talking despite the fact they may use disclaimers, announce their topic, or tell bad jokes. Remember, spiritual gifts are "given for the benefit of those who love me and keep all my commandments, and him that seeketh so to do"[2].

When someone gets up to speak, we should assume they have sought inspiration to share with someone in the congregation, and we must ask ourselves, "Did they receive it for me?" We came to learn and hear what they say, so we can ask, "What do I need at this time?" Who doesn't need to be reminded of faith, repentance, tithing, or any other gospel principle that repeats through the wards of the world. To move forward on the covenant path, we all need gentle reminders to stay the course. As we approach each opportunity to listen with humility and acknowledge the sincere, albeit imperfect, efforts of others, our Sunday worship will be filled with added power and inspiration[3].

The 2% Principle:

Next time at church I will _____

_____

_____

_____

_____

_____

122

Small Summary -Listening must be the skill we practice the most-	
Avoid These Traps	Try These Tips
• *When you hear the topic announced you say, "another talk on ____ " and you stare off into oblivion.*	• *Focus on Christ and Cultivate the assumption that every speaker in our wards or branches is trying, since we all still need to improve*
• *You focus on the flaws and miss the topic*	• *Assume every speaker sought revelation for you*
• *You start to focus on other things until the next speaker goes up*	• *Have the mindset of "I never [heard a speaker] I couldn't learn something from"*

References/Resources:

1. Deseret News, March 31, 2009, "General Conference profile: President Henry B. Eyring"

2. Doctrine and Covenants 46:9

3. Ensign, April 1981, "A Lesson from My Conscience: Learning to Listen in Church," John A. Green

4. Ensign, January 1978, "The Six Best Talks I Ever Heard," Thomas W. Ladanye

Giving Feedback to Those Who Spoke

"Examine what is said and not who speaks."
- African Proverb

When my daughter Emma spoke in church for the first time, she was very nervous; she did a good job for a twelve-year-old who wrote her own talk. Before she spoke, she got some suggestions from me and my wife, yet the ideas were hers, and she used the examples we offered that she identified with. After the meeting, we had a number of people who told us and her that she'd done a great job. This praise is fine, yet if too often repeated, it becomes a phrase that does not mean much because it is not specific.

Don't get me wrong, sometimes we don't have enough time to communicate more specific praise as the person who spoke is walking past us, and we just see them out of the corner of our eye. I also understand that sometimes the person that spoke is trying to avoid people because they don't want the attention, and, even though their talk is done, they still want to shrink into the corner for the rest of their time at church. Sometimes, "Hey, good job," is all we can say as they walk by. But, with a little creativity, we can share our own personal experiences with the one that spoke.

About an hour after we got home, my daughter got calls from three different neighbors telling her what they learned and what example she used that they enjoyed. Two days later she got a card in the mail from the neighbor that lives three doors down from us stating similar comments about what they learned personally.

Getting feedback on a talk can be meaningful, especially if it contains examples of personal insights into what the hearer learned. "Let one speak at a time and let all listen unto [their] sayings, that when all have spoken that all may be edified of all"[1]. When a speaker hears how they helped edify someone else, this can prompt additional motivation and confidence for the next time that they are asked to share in church. If we listen to talks for that personal edification, then we can become inspired on how to give that message of gratitude to the one that spoke to us.

Consider how the quick statement of, "I loved that personal example you gave; it really made me think," can have a positive impact, even briefly shared in passing. The phone calls after church only lasted a few seconds for our neighbors yet had a lasting impression on my daughter and us as her parents. A small note prepared in the meeting can easily be slipped to the person as they walk by you in the hall. Emma still has the card in her box of remembrance; something like that can last forever and can be a great reminder that someone listened to and was touched by your message.

Giving specific feedback is another way to be "anxiously engaged in a good cause, and do many things of [our] own free will, and bring to pass much righteousness"[2].

The 2% Principle:

Next time at church I will _____

_____
_____
_____
_____
_____

Small Summary *-Listen to be edified,* *tell the speaker how they lifted you-*
Try These Tips
• *What Did You Like, What Did You Learn?* • *What example or story got into your heart?* • *Write a note or send a letter* • *Make a call or text a message*

References:

1. Doctrine and Covenants 88:122
2. Doctrine and Covenants 58:27

Prepare for Sacrament Services Like General Conference

*"A great thought begins by seeing something differently,
with a shift of the mind's eye."*
- Albert Einstein

I have a good friend that opened my eyes to creating amazing sacrament services. She has a journal with every talk given in her ward for the past several years. She says it is not a lot of writing: she just puts down the date, the speaker's name, and then one or two lines of thoughts from each talk. It only takes a few seconds for each talk, yet it has blessed her life immensely. I asked her, "Where did you get this idea?" Her answer was, "I realized I do this for General Conferences, so why not for weekly worship?"

She referenced an email from the church with an article by President Uchtdorf about preparing for the upcoming General Conference, and she took its advice. She got a lot out of conference that year, so she started doing it each Sunday and has found similar results (Ensign, September 2011, "General Conference—No Ordinary Blessing," By President Dieter F. Uchtdorf)[1]. Here are the bullet points of the article and how she adapted them:

- Members of the Church are entitled to personal revelation as they listen to and study the inspired words spoken at general conferences (or in sacrament meeting services).

- Don't discount a message merely because it sounds familiar.
- The words spoken at general conferences (or sacrament meeting services) should be a compass that points the way for us during the coming months (or weeks).

Another article is also referenced in the gospel library app under General Conference (Ideas to Prepare to Participate in General Conference)[2]. This article highlights the following points:

- Ask questions and look for answers.
- Open your heart and mind and hear Him.
- Learn more about the special witnesses (or the testimonies of people in your ward or branch) of Jesus Christ.

As she comes to church prepared to listen, she finds any talk can bring an answer, any talk can invite revelation, and her favorite talks are by those who are simply trying and doing their best, without excuses.

These little, quiet moments of pondering during any talk have brought to my friend the promise made by Boyd K Packer about the blessings reverence brings to our services; he stated:

> While we may not see an immediate, miraculous transformation, as surely as the Lord lives, a quiet one will take place. The spiritual power in the lives of each member and in the Church will increase. The Lord will pour out his Spirit upon us more abundantly. We will be less troubled, less confused. We will find revealed answers to personal and family problems without all the counseling which we seem now to need[3].

Another article offers counsel on how to apply conference talks to your life and change without becoming overwhelmed. These same principles can also be used weekly in our Sacrament services ("4 Ways to Avoid 'General Conference Overwhelm'" By Alison Wood)[4].

Here are the highlighted points:
- Ask the Lord to tell you one thing you're doing right.
- Honestly evaluate yourself.
- Pray to know what to focus on
- Start small.

There are many sources where we can learn the gospel and find answers to our questions and to our prayers. When we are proactive and come with the intent to learn, we can receive answers through our individual studies and weekly services.

The 2% Principle:

Next time at church I will _____

_____

_____

_____

_____

Small Summary *-You always get out of something* *what you put into it-*	
Avoid These Traps	Try These Tips
• *Wait six months to get your answers* • *Discount messages because they sound familiar* • *Allow distractions to occupy your attention*	• *Actively listen each week to receive revelation* • *Learn through intentional practice how you hear Him* • *Learn about the people in your ward or branch and their testimonies of Jesus Christ*

References/Resources:

1. Ensign, September 2011, "General Conference—No Ordinary Blessing," Dieter F. Uchtdorf

2. Ideas to Prepare to Participate in General Conference

3. Ensign, November 1991, "Reverence Invites Revelation," Boyd K. Packer

4. "4 Ways to Avoid 'General Conference Overwhelm'," Alison Wood

Teaching Children to Speak in Church

*"Train up a child in the way he should go:
and when he is old, he will not depart from it."*
- Proverbs 22:6[1]

The principles included in the chapters of this book relate to both adults and children alike. As a parent or a teacher, you can adapt any of the principles to the children in your life. This chapter can help you focus on the right messages your child needs to hear as they prepare the talk, give the talk, and step down from the microphone. You want to teach them the right mindset and help them build both self-esteem and self-efficacy.

Self-Esteem: (Self-Efficacy vs. Self-Esteem 5:08)2

This is described as a person's belief in their worth and ability to impact others around them, to believe that they matter, even in a small way. This is especially important in your or your child's small circle of influence. As a child grows, so does their circle of influence, or in other words, the world around them. So help them build a belief that they matter, help them know they impacted someone, even if it is you, or you can arrange for someone to come up to them later and give them feedback[3]. The messages your child needs to hear are that their words meant something to someone else and that the time and anxiety they invested into speaking were worth it.

Self-Efficacy: (Importance of Self-Efficacy 4:02)4

This is described as a person's confidence in their ability to do something, to set a goal, and to believe they will achieve it. As a child learns they can speak in front of people, they learn a skill that can set them apart from other people as they grow older. The ability to stand out by doing something others don't want to do can water the seed of self-efficacy in a child, and they will not depart from it, if it continues to be nourished. There are four ways to help build self-efficacy:

1. Mastery Experiences

If we help our children set a goal and push through the hard emotions or doubts, they will enjoy the end result and want to do it again.

2. Social Modeling

As they see their parents or other members of their congregation speaking with confidence and enjoying it, they will also believe it is an attainable goal for themselves Ensign, August 2010, "Delivering an Effective Talk," Marcus Sheridan[5].

3. Social Persuasion

When a person is told that they have the capability and that others believe in them, especially if it is someone they look up to, they will be willing to take those risks that lead to success.

4. Master Their Physiology

If children learn how to manage their emotions and how to challenge the self-doubts they have, they will eventually learn how to talk themselves through the hard situations that come their way in the future (Self-Esteem, Self-Efficacy, and Locus of Control 7:59)6.

As they build self-esteem and self-efficacy, there builds a new inner-dialogue inside of their heads as they step down from the microphone. They can start to say to themselves, "Wow, now that I did that, what else can I do?" rather than say, "Phew, I'm glad that's over with"[7].

The 2% Principle:

I can help children learn to gain confidence by _____

_____

_____

_____

_____

_____

Small Summary	
-Shape the future speakers of the church-	
Self-Esteem:	Self-Efficacy:
Help them see their words matter to others by complimenting with specific things you liked	Help them develop confidence in their abilities by setting goals and accomplishing them
Help them see their impact on others and that their effort was worth it	Teach them to say "Now that I have done that, what else can I do?"
Self-worth with NO self-efficacy = Magical thinking, talk a big game but can't deliver.	
Self-efficacy with NO self-worth = Feelings of being an imposter, they shrink away from things they are capable of doing	
Self-worth + self-efficacy = Resilience, patience, mastery of emotions, willingness to do hard things, ability to set goals and believe they can achieve them.	

References/Resources:

1. Proverbs 22:6

2. YouTube: Cameron R. Armstrong - Live a Life Worth Living Q&A Ep. 04 Part 01 "What is Self- Concept?"- Self-Esteem

3. See Part Six: Giving Feedback to Those Who that Spoke

4. YouTube: Cameron R. Armstrong - Live a Life Worth Living Q&A Ep. 04 Part 02 "What is Self- Concept?"- Self-Efficacy

5. Ensign, August 2010, "Delivering an Effective Talk," Marcus Sheridan

6. YouTube: Cameron R. Armstrong - Live a Life Worth Living Q&A Ep. 05 "How do I take control of my life?"- Locus of Control

7. Albert Bandura: Self-Efficacy for Agentic Positive Psychology

8. The Friend, June 2003, "Isaac's Talk," Dawn Nelson

9. The Friend, April 2001, "The Talk," T. S. Hettinger

10. "Speaking in Church," From the Life of President Heber J Grant

11. Here is a video of a young boy that has both self-esteem and self-efficacy and how the two together help him stay resilient and overcome cancer treatment: YouTube: Nine-Year-Old Fan Teaches J.J. Watt About True 'Will Power' | My Wish

Concluding Thoughts

About four months into my mission for The Church of Jesus Christ of Latter-day Saints, I was standing in a group of eight missionaries when the bishop came up to us and said, "We had a speaker call in sick; can I have one of you give a talk today?" I remember all of us looking around and hoping one of the others would volunteer. I distinctly remember my companion, Elder Jason Judy, stepping up and saying, "Sure Bishop, I got you." The rest of us, including the Bishop, gave out a sigh of relief. Because Elder Judy was my companion, I sat on the stand with him, and he gave a great talk and everyone complimented him on his words. I was also impressed and reflected upon how the rest of us were afraid, yet he stepped up confidently.

I learned a lesson from Elder Judy that day. Public speaking is intimidating for everyone, but if I learned to enjoy that skill, it would set me apart from everyone else, as it did for him that day. Developing any talent helps you stand out from the crowd. Sharing our talents will lead to better confidence in yourself, better confidence in your abilities, and give you greater opportunities in the future.

As time moved on, whenever opportunities to speak arose I began to step up to give a talk, no matter who was in the room. Even if other missionaries had been out longer than me, or adults with more experience were present, I made it a race to see that I could volunteer first. After seeing the relief on the hesitant faces of the others, and hearing the compliments I received after I spoke, I realized I could do this hard thing despite my youth and inexperience.

I learned that enjoying public speaking became something I could do anywhere: commenting in a Sunday school lesson, a presentation in school, leading a meeting in church or at work, welcoming everyone to a family gathering before we eat, or any number of opportunities.

I hope that through the principles, mindsets, and tips from this book, you too can gain the confidence and power identified below, by one of the greatest speakers of all time:

> "Of all the talents bestowed upon men,
> none is so precious as the gift of oratory.
> He who enjoys it
> wields a power more durable than that of a great king.
> He is an independent force in the world.
> Abandoned by his party, betrayed by his friends,
> stripped of his offices,
> whoever can command this power
> is still formidable."
> ***-Winston Churchill***[1]

Yet, as powerful the gift of oratory may be on its own, it is nothing compared to linking this gift with your humility and faith in the Lord Jesus Christ. With him, we "can do all things,"[2]. Elder Bednar summarizes our gifts with faith in the Savior this way:

> This simply means that we trust in the Savior as our Advocate and Mediator and rely on His merits, mercy, and grace during the journey of life. As we are steadfast in coming unto Christ and are yoked with Him, we receive the cleansing, healing, and strengthening blessings of His infinite and eternal Atonement[3].

References:

1. Anthony McCarten, 2017, "Darkest Hour: How Churchill Brought England Back from the Brink"

2. Philippians 4:13

3. Liahona May 2022 "But We Heeded Them Not" David A. Bednar

*"He who only does what he can
will always remain what he is."*
- Henry Ford

*"The worst speech you'll ever give
will be far better
than the one you never give."*
-Fred Miller

About the Author

Cameron Armstrong is a licensed clinical social worker helping people overcome their mental health challenges. He learned to overcome his own anxiety related to public speaking as he served a full-time mission to Chicago and later playing live in bands. He lives in Utah with his wife and three children.

He still finds joy in playing the drums.

Made in the USA
Monee, IL
06 April 2023

30874886R00085